# DIVORCE
# 2
# DIVORCE

# DIVORCE 2 DIVORCE
## Your Heart in Your Home

## Alok Kr
The World's original
Thinker-cum-Writer

authorHOUSE®

*AuthorHouse™ UK Ltd.*
*500 Avebury Boulevard*
*Central Milton Keynes, MK9 2BE*
*www.authorhouse.co.uk*
*Phone: 08001974150*

*First published by AuthorHouse 8/22/2011*

*ISBN: 978-1-4567-8470-6 (sc)*
*ISBN: 978-1-4567-8471-3 (e)*

To my Late Father who, despite all his hardships in his life, had ensured doing his best to provide us, i.e. his children, the most needed thing that a human being must have, against all odds and in any circumstances, i.e. "Education". To lead a life of respect and understanding, this is the most desirable nutrient in anyone's life on our Mother Earth.

To my each brethren, living or dead, on this Mother Earth who could not lead a life of respect and understanding for no fault of their own.

To my those brethren who want to lead such a life as would give them the satisfaction of not only living here on this ever beautiful Earth but also that they want to contribute their level best in spite of their handicap or lack of resources.

## *Epigraph*

"I am thankful to all those who said NO to me. It's because of them I did it myself".

(Albert Einstein)

ईश्वराणां वचः सत्यं तथैवाचरितं क्वचित ।
तेषां यत स्ववचोयुक्तं बुद्धिमान्स्तत समाचरेत ।।

i.e. "The teachings and preachings of the God are just and true. One ought to follow them; one ought to act or behave according to them. But their action or behavior is not always just, true and imitable. The action or behavior of the God which follows or is acted and behaved according to their teachings and preachings; that very action or behavior ought to, rather must, be followed and accepted, imbided and imitated."

स्त्री-पुमांसौ सम्परिष्वक्तौ, स इममेवात्मानं द्वेधा ।
ड्पातयत, ततः पतिश्च पत्नीचाभवताम ।।

i.e. "Woman and Man are; originally, fundamentally, principally; one, interwoven, unison, unitary. The God divided Himself into two, quantitatively and qualitatively, equal parts. And those very parts, i.e. the outcome of the bifurcation, came to be known as and became WOMAN and MAN or WIFE and HUSBAND."

**SWAGATAM**

**/**

**WELCOME**

to

**A World of original Thinking**

**&**

**Sharing the Fragrance of Love**

**in**

**Our Homes**

# Contents

# Foreword

This book, **Divorce 2 Divorce**, is dedicated to a subject that has more facets than a diamond. To write a foreword on the subject of family togetherness and values is to state the obvious in that what could be more important than the bonds that keep a unit together.

However, as other influences erode these values we discover, much to our horror, that our grasp of the vital role the family plays in our lives is slipping and we are gradually splintering from the larger family of the mid twentieth century to the nuclear family of the 21st century to the lack of capacity to see it through and even finding it difficult to maintain the equilibrium of nurturing a loving family. That is when you realize it is necessary to raise a warning flag and this book is such a warning.

Which is why I feel privileged to touch upon the various aspects of why it has become necessary to address our weaknesses and reinforce our strengths.

Take the sanctity of marriage. Today divorce is acceptable. Indian society has allowed for it. People get married. They do not want to try hard to make it work. The coming together of two families is now shrunk to survival of two individuals.

It is like the flow of water. Parents have this unqualified desire to see their children's pursuit of happiness is constant and incessant.

One of the major milestones is to ensure that they are happily married at some reasonable point. There is little so devastating for parents growing into their winter years than to have their children walk the shards of shattered wedlock and come home.

Marriage becomes the first fallen jump and probably the largest. For parents per se, the wedding of a son and daughter is the acme of their investment in love and other more material tangibles. Along comes the son or daughter and cheerfully wrecks the planning with a mind of his or her own and the parents are aghast. They must now either shriek their indignation or, for the sake of appearances, dredge for virtue in the alien find and discover much to approve, even as they fervently hope their child will see sense.

The scenery is breathtaking, the atmosphere is crisp and stimulating, but if you don't pace yourself you run out of breath. The trick is to remember it is all uphill and you have to work at it, every little step of the way.

It is our duty to protect our customs and traditions and I never cease to be awed by the cavalier fashion in which the new generation dismisses them for the ketchup and chips culture that has overwhelmed everything else.

I use the word sometimes again. Sometimes, I feel alienated by my own strong feelings. It is so easy to be misunderstood when all I say is protect your antecedents. Not at the expense of someone else but with mutual love, respect and courtesy to everybody else.

It is so difficult to do that we end up perverting the concept of cultural integrity. I fear the fear more than anything else. That my children's children will not know who they are or what those roots mean to them. In this instant world, culture has been reduced to the level of coffee and become a light-hearted element in our lives.

Those who advocate the crossing of the lines without reservation sound like they are endowed with great largesse and generosity of spirit. But in their keenness to create this oneness they destroy what makes this world so special.

Across the board, rich or poor, the desire for possessions has washed away much of our tolerance and affection. It is our major motivation and corrupts the sense of belonging that the old family values demanded. Courtesy, respect for elders, love, they have been corroded and if this effort can remind us of what we now see as something that we could lose, it is necessary to recognize the threat.

Greed manifests itself as the top value. Love has become commercial and is equated with what can be obtained by way of money, wealth, property, like a commodity on sale. Brothers and sisters increasingly go to war. Parents are marginalized in their dotage.

By the same token we do not have another precious gift to give anymore; time.

But all is not lost. So long as the arts have people like Alok Kumar who put on paper the intricacies and importance of family and underscore the power and majesty of kith and kin perhaps the message of solidarity can be revived.

This book will then have done its work and done it well.

Bikram Vohra, Editorial Board, Khaleej Times

# Preface

## "My Heart Resonates"

Old head on young shoulder! You are young if you feel young. Being young is good. Still better is staying young and healthy.

I was born into a business-cum-agriculture family in a remote rural village called Rajauli in a state called Bihar in India. As a kid I was playful but perhaps, something more. I grew up, not only playing, but experiencing and going through things that a kid would be least interested in. I think, right since my childhood, I always looked for something more, than what was external, in everything I saw.

When I grew up, I wanted to be an Engineer, Administrator etc. Fortunately, I think, I was less fortunate to get the kind of formal education that each one of us dreams about. My father was a lawyer. I would often lay my hands on the books that concern me least and my father most. More than that, I would go through them as well without wasting my time. Apart from my curriculum books, I would try to finish books, at the earliest, that would pertain to others.

I think formal and class book education may turn one into an achieved academician. But to be successful, we need something more. It depends upon our hobby or interest. Formal and class book education may land one into a high paying job or employment. To be able to contribute something purposefully to the community, we rather need much more than formal upbringing and education. That makes one unconventional and cut above the rest. The biggest achievement for an individual, in my opinion, is maintaining the originality, fresh-ness and uniqueness of a kid who, in spite of seeing everything happening around himself/herself, remains as fresh as the morning.

Being able to remain, while exiting, as origi-nal and fresh an individual as entering into a career; Employed or Self-employed, any job or organization; is a difficult choice or outcome to expect. But if we are able to do that I think this ought to be termed as the greatest of all achievements in our lives. As time passes, we all change as Change is perennial. But maintaining the freshness throughout our life, I think, will be a good thing to happen. Freshness of mind, body and character is invaluable.

I think our freshness, of mind, body and character, should be a necessary ingredient in our daily life as well. That will keep us committed, dedicated and motivated to whatever we do or are required to do. This is all the more needed in our marital life too. Freshness and Intensity in the beginning of our job or relationship endear us to people around. We will carry ourselves to the fruition of our endeavours if we are able to not only maintain but rather reinforce it during the course of our journey into that job or relationship. How do we do that? Inside each one of us, there is an invisible thing called FILTER and we need to discover and activate that.

Women are another important creature that provides freshness in our human lives. Without them, I think, this world has no meaning. They are the elixir, rather the world itself, for a number of individuals and families. The most beautiful aspect of their life is they don't carry anything to their next birth or life. They pay back their debts to the Mother Earth by giving births and fulfill their debt burden. If we follow closely and properly, we are taught a number of lessons out of their existence. As males, we do not have this facility to pay back the debts that we owe to our Mother Earth. We can do that but only by doing something good and benignant to our Mother Earth by saving our (re)sources. Let us leave it to the choice of each of our brethren living with us.

Right since my childhood I am carrying a belief that each one of us living here on the earth carries some purpose of life. I hope I am not wrong and am able to carry it to the last breathe of my life. That encourages me to not consider any individual disrespectfully and take him/her not only seriously but also evince proper interest to encourage achieving more and more in his/her life. I think that is what we try to address through our Individual or Corporate Social Responsibility and Inclusive Growth. So many people around us are always our sources of inspiration and help us learn and unlearn every single moment of our life. If we really want to improve the quality of our lives, we should have contagious desire to learn from the mistakes committed by others rather than committing the same mistake ourselves.

Some important things key to our existence on the Mother Earth I am going to share now. 5 things external, present in our nature, and 5 things internal, inside our bodies, we must take care of to lead a durable life of satisfaction and achievement. Please do have a guess! What are they? ASFEW i.e. Air, Sky, Fire, Earth and Water are the 5 most important external things and THEEN i.e. Tongue, Hands, Eyes, Ears and Nose are the 5 most important internal things. Can anyone dispute the importance of these 10 elementary things? Probably not! It goes without saying that we must not only take care of these 10 things but also employ them judiciously and cost-effectively.

I have scripted this book hoping to share some of our important topics that concern us most today. And hoping that together we can make this world, a different one, a livable and enjoyable one where we share our thoughts and moments freely and purposefully. This is the first of a series of 3 books. Hopefully after it, we shall be sharing some of our important thoughts and moments together through the second one titled; **"Freedom Unfinished"** in the near future.

I request everyone to go through and enjoy reading this book. Let us love and be loved!

# Breathlessness

"There will be plenty
of time to sleep
when you are dead.
Life is for living. So wake up and perform".

(Benjamin Franklin)

On this prepossessing earth, a variety of natural and unnatural creations or creatures exist. Out of which majority have some limitations. And they know about their limitations; to wit, in respect of their very existence, in respect of their very nature of construction, in respect of their usefulness. But many other creations or creatures do not have any knowledge about their limitations, nor do they bother to be acquainted in this respect. Quite similarly someone's desire or longing or imagination is one of such creations that do not have any idea of its limitations in the aforesaid respects. It awfully rattles our, almost each one of us, hearts, and compels our mental sedateness and soberness to vacillate.

It also drives our decisions from one end to another, from everything to nothing and from nothing to everything. At some places it does violate i.e. cross over the boundary of dignity of our being humans whereas at some other places it does not do so. But the invisible living being who is above all of us, who is omnipotent, no such problems beset Him. No such happening occurs to Him at all. He has not only time and again successfully fulfilled His desires or imaginations but also has perfectly secured His dignity. That is why His every creation, excessively minute or huge howsoever may be, purely satiates us, delights us to an unlimited extent; drives us to the acme of our inborn feelings.

In this picturesque world created by Him every creation, whether natural or unnatural, is liked or disliked according to its merits or demerits, its usefulness or harmfulness. Fondness or hatefulness, for someone or something, is the very reason for the increase or decrease in one's or its relative importance. Both kind of creations can be identified and separated from one an-other with the help of their respective natures. Both of them with the help of their respective qualities force us to feel their presence. He is the one to whom all prayers are made who richly deserves so because of being at once the benevolent and the omnipotent. His every single direct or indirect, minute or huge creation of this very magnificent world has undoubtedly been created or brought forth with the sole and pure purpose of doing a serviceable gen-eral welfare to one and all inhabiting this ever attractive world. Also, time and circumstances are the factors which do have a helping hand in increasing or decreasing the significance and usefulness of all the creations.

To earn curse or to be cursed is something of a desire or an imagination to be perhaps not cropping up in anyone's mind, not even in one's dreams. Hardly any single creature in this world does have the necessary courage and honesty to accept and display itself, as the pure source or cause of a blemish, blur or a curse. Doing this is a whiff of being great by nature as well as existence. As we all know fully well that greatness approves of all round amelioration and prosperity in respect of the goings-on concerning every natural or unnatural creation of this world. And it is a great pleasure indeed that our mother earth is purely fortunate in this sense. Reaching or acquiring a good manner, character or opinion is really a tedious and tiresome excursion but rather more strenuous, for one, is to be like that wholesomely for the most while.

The creator of this very beautiful and fascinating world has created many more innumerable things, including us humans, which we experience in our day-to-day life. With the help of His creations, mortal as well as immortal, He fulfils His plans at the relevant times with proper creations making them play as pawns and puppets. This very tradition has been uninterruptedly continuing for the countless centuries. Whenever there is a sudden and great change in times or circumstances, in the past or present, we find in brevity[1] that

---

1    In brief.

almost every single creature, living or dead, of this world has also contributed in some form or the other according to its significance. Similarly we, being the wisest creature next only to that indirect God, have also till now created innumerable things with the help of His creations for our comfort and suitability as well as for our destruction and uneasiness.

Creations, we all might agree, are unarguably the fulfillment of the ambitions of the determined people. As is rightly said, "Necessity is the mother of invention." That is why whenever there is a dire need of something, the ambitious and determined people join their hands to come on top of the pan. Whatever we see or feel around us, natural or unnatural, significant or insignificant, mortal or immortal, all fall under this category. Almost everything on this prepossessing earth has been bestowed gratis upon us by the benevolent creator.

With the help of these creations we have been able to create or bring about so many things, acceptable as well as unacceptable, attractive as well as repulsive, pleasing as well as annoying, that we twinkle our eyes in surprise for good and benign achievements and in despise for bad and malign ones. But in spite of all accomplishments one thing, that is quite obvious, is that we have not been able to make good and full use of everything imparted to us. We have constantly been making our living along with the surroundings acrid and bitter by our erroneous and unhandy use of good many things.

What an irony that we have been producing evils against good, making or bringing forward malefactors against benefactor and yet hope to be happy and prosperous. This kind of strange and outlandish[2] attitude is inextricably prevalent or pinned in almost all of us, whether high or low, small or big, poor or rich. In fact, this attitude dominates us. Well the goody fact is that we are only humans and as we know, "To err is human." Perhaps it applies to most of us. That is why when one errs most of the people do not pay their slightest heed or attention, even at least for a jiffy, to that error. They just take and rate that error as wonted and jeer at the wrongful person and in the most cases we, too, mutely follow that error only to our detriment. But as

---

2   Uncommon or Unusual

we know excess of anything is bad and hence there must be a limit to everything, especially opprobrious ones.

We have been descended on this magnificent earth by the almighty purely to help continue the unceasing and well established tradition of running accurately this world and work as efficient carriers and then to hand over to our descendents a world free, so much as possible, of any kind of hostility, acerbity and frustration so as to have an elbowroom for them to do their worth. After thanking the almighty for this great boon i.e. descending us on this magnificent earth and without wasting this golden opportunity we should rise to the occasion to prove His decision's appropriateness to oblige Him. This is our responsibility and duty, too.

Responsibility, because in handing over this magnificent world to our descendents, it must be suitable and appropriate enough to be livable to them. If we prove to be unsuccessful in doing so and it does not befit them well, they would accurse and call us a bane and boorish generation on that established chaste tradition maintained by countless generations.

And a duty because we too have to live in and before we go off the scene, it is our birthright to have an agreeable and pleasing atmosphere around us. The need arises also out of sheer selfishness that we must work for the betterment of the atmosphere around us. Moreover, our descendents would not know the value and necessity of good and agreeable surroundings around themselves and hence might shirk away from shouldering the chaste responsibility of bettering this already prepossessing world and then a distortion in that long established and unceasing tradition would come up or surface in spite of our full knowledge only to make us shed tears.

We enjoy being here and hence are also reciprocally bound to do so. We have already reached into the Space and it is now an old story as we had first landed there at the Moon some 55 years back. To add another feather to our cap the new thing is that we are having conventions and contemplations and maneuvering and hoping too, to establish a manned colony out there at Mars latest by 2020-2025 i.e. by another 10-15 years more. It is indeed a high ambition and if comes true, an extremely envious and unexpected achievement for the whole mankind. But before having such a colony we shall have to have a satisfactory basic knowledge about the circumstances and surroundings out there and in order to have them according to our suitability we shall have to amend ourselves so as to be inhabitable there.

But before jumping to have any discussion about there we are fixed to properly think over our existence and identity here. We are inextricably perplexed with the questions of the following kinds concerning these issues. Are we doing our jobs satisfactorily and performing well here? That too, for our safety and longevity? Are we happy and satisfied with the things and surroundings we have been having here? And if not, are we then working and labouring for their all round upliftment so as to have a hopeful future awaiting us and our descendents as well?

Answers to all these questions are presently not in our bags because one thing which is certain is that we are really not happy and satisfied with the things happening here and hence we are dutiful to labour up to make the air around us clear and dapper off all the evils or ills so much as possible to have a scintilla of a hopeful future for ourselves. We are being constantly puzzled, perplexed and harassed with the quagmirish[3] results one after another of the ills of our own wrong doings. Thanks to our above-mentioned strange and outlandish attitude! We would have a separate discussion, in another edition, about the conspicuous evils or ills that have been having a devastating effect on our individual, familial and social atmosphere with an extremely polluting result inside as well as outside our homes.

Apart from a host of natural and man-made disasters happening across the globe, the most important of these conspicuous an evil is AIDS i.e. Acquired Immuno Deficiency Syndrome. It has been having very serious and destabilizing effects on our minds, our bodies, our children, our teenagers, our youths, our homes and our societies and what not. It is reducing our homes to a dwindled state wherein we constantly feel and foresee our identity and existence in a dire danger.

---

3    A difficult or precarious situation

We are fully familiar with the fact that one's own home is the mainstay i.e. supreme amongst all, of the stoppages one can avail of in one's life. We, along with our scions, love to spend our hours in our respective homes with happiness and peacefulness. Each one of us here on earth wholeheartedly longs for a home of his/her own imagination wherein he/she could live and enjoy his/her life with his/her family. We build and erect our homes with such hopes with an eye on our capacities. We spend so much as our capacities allow us to have a home in respect of our needs. Just a little bit of pondering over and we jump to the conclusion that right from our birth we live and grow in our respective homes and continue to be therein till our last breath departs us.

All this means that we take or are given birth in our respective homes; we grow up in our respective homes; we get our first school-ing in our respective homes. We get off this worldly scene only after thanking many a time this prepossessing world right from within our very own respective homes. Moreover bread, clothing and shelter are the unavoidable and fundamental requirements for each one of us, which nobody has the authority to deprive of. We love to be in our homes in any kind of moment, whatsoever. We adjourn to our respective homes whenever we feel tired, worrisome or perturbed with something. When everything comes to a halt by the dead of night we stay in our respective homes and go to roost therein. When something catches us hazardous or endangers our identity and existence we hastily take recourse in our respective homes because we feel safe therein.

Whether it is piping hot or downpouring rain or chilling cold everyone's ready choice to take harbour in falls upon his/her own home. Whether it is nature's disastrous behaviour or a manmade disaster one's ready answer to scamper away to be safe and secure is one's own closet or home. We spend most part of our lives at our respective homes. In fact, one's own home is the best and most suitable place to have a peaceful and happy tarrying and pure breathing. That is why we search for our happiness and peacefulness in our own respective homes. An example would be sufficient to support this claim. When one is dishoused or deprived of one's shelter, one fights out to one's last breath to have re-access to one's lost house or shelter. Thus conclusively it is a dead known fact that everyone's safest in-place and harbour is his/her own home consisted of four walls, whether small or big.

But despite knowing fully well all these facts the questions which might abuzzingly[4] sprout up in our minds after having a philosophical look at the present individual, familial and social problems and predicaments is that "what we have been doing with our homes now a days". Whether we have been working for its safety, stability and soundness or for its weakness and destruction? At one hand we have been creating new homes with the idea of arraying them with newly wed couples. And on the other we have been constantly demolishing our well erect old ones with the help of the painful practice of separation i.e. Divorce only to infuse restlessness, bitterness and frustration among the inhabitants of the homes as well as the society.

Now a days our homes are rollicking with an unknown fear coupled with its dire consequences because of which we are not

---

4    Reminding violently

feeling sure of their as well as our unity and stability. It seems as if we are being married only to be seen and counted as divorced or single hood. And this very ill tradition has been playing a supportive role in increasing and quantifying the deadly AIDS. Owing to all this we are now inextricably fixed in a foggy and indecisive atmosphere. This kind of confusing and quaggy situation provides a dependable staircase with the help of which it has been extending and stretching out its arms over more and more areas by leaps and bounds for the last few years becoming omnipresent. AIDS has been having a hazardous effect on our children, our teenagers, and our youths along with we elders. It has been annihilating our homes as well as all the hopes of our future. Having a putrefying attitude towards our homes, our society will be a killing one.

With all the seriousness it needs to be gravely combated and contained. We must not allow it to go by mocking or jeering at us. It is all just like the accursed blurs or blemishes on our homes, which has been exerting its fullest backdoor influence to topple our very existence and identity. As we all know fully well that the blurs or blemishes, whether on our face, family, home, society or social reputation, are things expected only to be begrudged and done away with. That is why at the first instance itself we try to nip it in the bud to make it disappear from our homes and societies. And for this each one of us is expected to come forward to with one's full individual capabilities. It has been so shockingly rattling our minds, bodies, homes and societies that we are condemned to have serious discussions, seminars, webinars and many more such things so as to be unapproachable and unassailable by it. If we really and truly care for ourselves, our offshoots i.e. the next generation, our homes, our societies and the surroundings around us then we shall have to have our attitudes and activities sincerely amended.

Perhaps we are all not ourselves today. We have, one by one, been bypassing the limits and boundaries of ours being humans and all this is what have been bemusing and bemiring us. We have become too much self-centered and careless about our identity and existence. There has been all round depreciation in moral as well as human values the world over. We have been unable to impose any kind of check upon all these departures and depredations, let alone the talks of having whiffs or any scintilla of success of amelioration in this respect. AIDS has been embittering, bemusing and fixing us in a predicament owing to which we are intolerably worried about our very existence and identity.

And so we are condemned to have a calculated and determined pondering over to adeptly work out some appreciable and effective usages to obviate it. Being its generator we are obliged, under obligation of residence, to do so. For this hellish and diabolical situation we are ourselves responsible and hence we could contemn with none except us alone. Now we shall again drive ourselves back to the much interesting topic of an assiduous and miraculous task of establishing a manned colony out there on Mars latest by 2020-2025 i.e. in another 10-15 years' time. The whole world is anxiously waiting to hear some words of success in this respect.

The questions that should come up or brew in everyone's mind are about their safety, soundness, stability and longevity as to upon what sort of terms or bases they would depend. Whether the homes out there will be safe, sound and independent of any kind of inappropriateness or speculations to which we are addicted here? In spite of the fact that we are no more safe and integrated on Mother Earth we are deliberately maneuvering to have such a colony out there. Here at one hand we are having the hottest topic of the century i.e. The Green House Effect or the Ozone Effect and on the other the deadliest topic i.e. The AIDS.

At one hand we are waffled with the man's harmful officious influence on the climate and on the other we are horrified with the man's harmful officious attitude towards the similitude creatures. At one hand we are recurrently receiving quaking shocks with the climatic revolutions fanning the waves against us and on the other we are being coercively vanquished with the officious attitude's revolutionary outbreak of diseases to subduing us. At one hand we have been incessantly receiving extinguishing droughts, floods, earthquakes and tsunamis and on the other the annihilating diseases like AIDS, Flues etc. In both the cases we are going to face a questionable existence in the next 50-100 years or so. We are being foundered with all our hands in the fanning waves or subduing diseases with the none-too-convincing hope against hope of to be again safely traced or pulled out. In spite of having no control, not even the slightest, over any system or unit, natural or unnatural, on this earth we are deliberately maneuvering to establish a manned colony out there in Space i.e. Antariksha[5].

We are doing nothing but playing mischievous pranks with ourselves and the whole of the mankind and demolishing our well built homes here with the inhabitants helplessly exposed to be treated with as would be wanted and liked by the so called hazardous side-effects. In the current situation, at one hand when we are not capable of providing any kind of dependable safety and stability to our own homes here on the Earth then how could we, on the other, provide such measures for our homes out there in the Space? Is there any guarantee that they, i.e. the homes,

---

5    Sanskrit word for the Space.

will ever be safe and sound out there? When we are not able to stabilize the future of our offshoots as well as ourselves due to the surroundings getting more and more tarred and acerbated here then how can we expect to have our existence and identity encouraging out there?

Homes, as we all know fully well, are the backbone of any society and hence they expect and need our best attention to be paid towards their safety, stability and longevity. It is true and proper that we must act for their amelioration in the sense of safety, stability, longevity and purity as well, to be happy and prosperous in the future. The environment inside as well as outside our homes has been becoming embittering and exasperating here, thanks to our own misdeeds. But the strangest is the fact that yet we hope of and promise about our homes in the Space to be safe and sound. This venomous and infernal situation must now be properly shoveled out or else we are only to sink more and more effacing our very existence and identity. Moreover one thing which should be hovering in everyone's mind is that when we are unsuccessful in maintaining and ameliorating the surroundings around us here, not altogether befitting and suitable to our living, then have we got any right or authority to spoiling or smothering the peaceful, so much as we know, surroundings out there?

Certainly we do have no such authority. We have already fore smothered the atmosphere out there thanks much to our heavily popularized STAR WARS programme, i.e. Strategic Defense Initiative. We shall only add fuel to the fire because we shall land those very people there who are, at present, here with us. And here, as we all know, we are arguably and questionably dependable and responsible, contributive and cooperative. Does it not mean then that it will be just like falling from the frying pan into the fire? Bearing in mind all these necessities we drive to the conclusion that we must first amend ourselves, our attitudes and activities, to have an agreeable and pleasing atmosphere inside and outside our homes here so that we could freely and cooperatively work together to have palmy⁶ days for us and our offshoots. This difficult and headstrong task

---

6    Prosperous or happy days

needs to be started right from within our own respective homes because these provide for us safest in-place to a peaceful and happy living. First and foremost, our homes need to be corrected and de-polluted, together with our attitudes and activities, as we are at once their upkeepers and dwellers. Only pure and upright home can provide for us elbowroom to play our respective contributory roles for the identity and longevity of the mankind.

For this, we shall have to correct and mould our people right from their birth. We shall have to impart to them such an education so as to be helpful to and desirable by their family, society and mankind as well. Bearing in mind this important aim we all need to doggedly work as only good and amicable homes with cooperative atmosphere can make or produce such kind of good and acceptable personalities.

It is PERSONALITY that defines a person; Personality is called a man or a woman or else we are just like an unknown vegetating creature that does not even know the purpose of its living. It was Personality that came to be known and earned celebrity status the world over which we are condemned to servilely remember even today. This world is full of such Personalities even now and naming a few will only leave too many to be desired. Such kind of celebrated and exclusive Personalities are possible today also provided that we are responsible, cooperative, impulsive and chastely industrious. These kinds of Personalities never teach us to be arrogant and aberrant. These kinds of Personalities play an important role in guiding the mankind to follow its right and conventional good path.

Hence we jump to the conclusion that everything good, teenless and impulsive emanates or shows its very first refulgence and fragrance from our own homes. Hope or despair, irrespective of its nature, rays out from our own homes. Thus we shall, first of all, have to amend ourselves, correct and de-pollute our homes so as to have expectations of producing such kind of impressive and great personalities. Only in good and understandingly cooperative homes we can expect of our offshoots to be happy and prospering in future, for anyone's very first school is one's very home where one is given birth in.

Now before we go on sharing further any more, one important topic calls for a place right here. We all might know fully well about two outstanding facts. First, we have been having a good and useful relationship among the countries of today the world over in spite of having several conflicting factors or matters of concern. Second, we long and opt for a high standard of living and brag of or take pride in our developed civilizations. Thus it automatically becomes our duty that we must jointly work to maintain that chaste traditional relationship to have more and more improvement in our living standards and the surroundings around us to have pure air to breathe and live in. Also, that our offshoots, along with we elders, deserve such standards and the surroundings as humanity empowers everyone to work to have all the basic requirements of life. Joint and cooperative association or organization is mostly needed for such works and that sort of association is the ultimate guest to an amicable enchainment.

Therefore we must first get justly enchained so as to be able to actively work for the betterment of the standards and surroundings around us as enchainment are the only solution and also the just track for doing so. In other ways too we long for enchainment, irrespective of its nature, because sans it hardly a single exertion or exercise, whether in the sense of one's family, society or country, is possible in this worldly world. In fact a good and unbreakable enchainment with mutual understanding makes one perfect, disciplined, cooperative, creative, gentle, confident, diligent, bold and what not. Most of us do love to put forth some words in its favour or its encomium. Only two kinds of creatures hate to be enchained and institutionalized and they are either devil or 4-legged animals because there is no meaning of enchainment to them and see where they are. Are they capable of putting forth any kind of definition for themselves? Can they solve the problems that concern them most, in respect of their existence, in respect of their identity? The answers to these questions are quite obvious.

The perfect example of a useful enchainment or institution, as we know, is the holy knot i.e. **"Marriage"**. Everyone, rather each one of us, loves to be enchained or enfettered for the good services of the mankind and that he/she readily puts aside everything that comes as hurdles in his/her way and produces obstructions. Moreover, to tackle with and contain the evils, most important AIDS, these kinds of chains are feasible and called for and hence to be, anyhow, put up with. But now a days, only to our dismay and annoyance, our very rightful and imitable institution or enchainment of marriage ends with dissolution as if meant for disunion. Whereas the true fact is that a good and amicable home with unbreakable enchainment between its dwellers i.e. Wife and Husband, can make or produce good, acceptable and amenable people who can do their worth in a befitting manner and help improve the living standards and the surroundings around us.

These kinds of homes can well train and educate their dwellers such as to how can one be perfect, lawful and helpful to oneself as well as the mankind and that how can one shoulder and deliver one's responsibilities. In spite of all kinds of improvements or developments the present state of affairs, nonetheless, does not appear to be encouraging. We shall continue to be in this problematic and merci-ful state or condition unless we amend our ac-tivities and attitudes and correct & de-pollute our homes as everything, even our existence and identity, depends on them. Thus after all we come to the final and ultimate decision that we must alleviate the present murky and boggy affairs that have been devastating our once safe and stabilized homes and rendering us homeless only to be channeled out to our doomsday. And it is high time we voluntarily come forward for the betterment of the sur-roundings inside as well as outside our homes so that there could be no more a shelter or room for the deadly AIDS.

Now we shall fall onto that initiative part of BREATHELESSNESS session where we shall have a thorough and calculated discussion about the main problem that has been rattling and having a distressing and disgusting effect on our homes.

It sounds little bit surprising that we our-selves have been proving quite of an an-noying factor to the whole of the mankind. We would first know fully well as to what is AIDS. In fact it has already secured its place as a household term or tool in each home in almost every nook and corner all over the world. AIDS, i.e. Acquired Immuno Deficiency Syndrome, today's most dreadful & quaking mal-outcome of our shortsighted, imprudent and obtrusive attitudes & deeds in the past and still on in the present, is the biggest and the most nonplussing[7] health problem of this century the mankind has been facing. What else, rather than it, would be more blemishful that we ourselves, thanks much to our own so called thoughts and deeds, have been proving quite of a curse and decayment for the very existence and identity of the whole of the mankind.

Our questionable, distrustful and prurient affairs are causing this fearsome disease which, without any doubt, proves or corroborates of us being at once selfish, uncontrollable and reprehensible. We are the mere spectators of our refractory deeds that have been helping us to live in a constant phobia of being evaporated to an unidentifiable existence. This mal-outcome i.e. AIDS is proving

---

7    A condition of perplexity in which one is unable to go, speak or act further.

like a coup-de-main on our homes as it has been smoothly endangering the very security, stability and amicability of the post-nuptial relationships. More than two decades have gone by since we had set out on our onset to contain and combat this spreading menace but we have achieved next to nothing. On the contrary, the number of the victims of this disease has been going up by leaps and bounds quite uninterruptedly. Now we shall have a scientific discussion of this deadly companion as to what are its aspects? Why so many people are falling into its net? What are the reasons behind this disease?

Unrestricted sexual intercourse or coition between a man and a woman is one of the most responsible or accountable factor behind it. Having such relationship with many a person at once, i.e. at one time, the uncontainable viruses of this disease take birth, which later mar our whole future, along with the present, by just fixing us in a dire state of cataclysm, confusion and darkness. Besides this, many more reasons do have or play a significant role in its genesis or protrusion. In the whole of Europe and North America, homosexual men and intravenous drug abusers are among its out-bursting net whereas in Africa the disease is predominantly spread through heterosexual intercourse, contaminated blood and from the infected mother to her foetus or baby. The internationally accepted term of this disease is Human Immuno Deficiency Virus (HIV) plus new variant recently isolated in patients with West African connections (HIV-II). About the number of victims of this disease high number of casualties has taken place almost everywhere like United States, Europe, United Kingdom, Asian countries and Australia. A calculated estimation put forth speaks that there will be an increasing trend all over the globe till we get a solution to it.

To tackle with this disease an approach based on humanity is advised wherein the processes like voluntary, free and easily accessible care, counseling and screening with self-restraint come. To this date the fact is that we have not yet been able to satisfyingly equip ourselves with a medicine to combat and contain its ever-spreading net. What an irony is this that even children, in spite of being at no fault, are now a days found infected with its virus. For, they are condemned to bear with the ill effects of the utterly shortsighted, officious and ignominious deeds of their respectful parents. They, i.e. the new-born babies and the children, are in all the senses quite incapable of solving or tackling with this kind of messy situation and hence are condemned to live constantly in a confusing and darkish phobia of being extinct in their foreseeable future.

AIDS is proving to be a blind alley wherein no concrete solution is in sight and yet we indulge in opprobrious and obtrusive sexual activities as if we have no eyes on our future. When our present generation is so much worried about and in a state of paranoia, what kind of future would be awaiting the next generation; one can have a complete guess. It has also been corroborated that AIDS is a subway-make-out of drug abusing also. Drug abusing too adds fuel to the fire in upsetting the whole set-up of the society. Shall we discuss here the aspects related to Drug Abuse? But before that let us go in detail what is it all about.

Most of us are just not acclimatized with drugs and do not even recognize or know anything by name. But we are horrified with the unsettling news that drugs have now found their ways even into our homes and schools. Drugs used as medicines for life saving purposes are really a necessity. But here we are discussing about the drugs that are used to destroy and vanquish us by both mind and body. The habits of drug abusing have now become a very serious problem for each one of us and calls for a determined and erudite attention to be paid so as to be combated and obfuscated because they are endangering our very existence and identity. This calls for utmost enthusiasm and ardour from us.

The causatives to this mal-practice are circumstantial as well as environmental but they all abide in our own homes. It is we who help or condemn our children, teenagers, youths and elders to become drug addicts only to gain our self interests or with some ulterior motives. The most imminent thing is that after becoming a drug addict what sort of feedback we receive in return, whether they ameliorate our living? Whether they strengthen our mental and physical disposition? Today's children, teenagers and youths are the future of our homes upon whose shoulders the responsibilities of tomorrow will fall. Drug addicts are also addicted to squander away their purse only to put themselves and the affairs of their families in danger, agonizing misery and a sense of confusion with something being received as feedback, the transient baseless sense of well being i.e. The Absolute Nothingness.

There are almost 190 countries in the whole world that face the uphill, arduous and exhaustive task of wiping it out so as to be happy and relieved off the mental pressure which is rather proving to be an Augean Stable[8]. Moreover, everyone's heart is throbbing today with the signs of the frightful fact that the disastrous and devastating effect of this disease on our society will reduce it to a society wherein only disease-begetting and problem-generating people dwell. Thus all these factors are joining their hands to make everything, i.e. the whole set-up, frenzied when we shall have no good and fragrant atmosphere inside as well as outside our homes. The dire need is of a good and amicable home with cordially

---

8    A condition or place marked by great accumulation of filth or corruption.

and emotionally knotted partners wherein we, along with our families and scions, can enjoy our living; can have breathable pure air. We must work for the betterment of our surroundings around us so as to be obviated of all kind of fears involved with the evils and then to hand over to our descendents a world they could brag of and take pride in it and in their one-up generation as well.

Thus, all in all, the choice falls upon a good, amicable, fragrant, understandably agreeable and pure atmosphere inside as well as outside our homes so as to be happy, peaceful and prosperous.

# Home

In the preceding chapter we have tried to share and throw light on the prevailing state of affairs, so far as our living on this Mother Earth is concerned. In the accompanying chapter we shall have a thorough and calculated elaboration about their harmful fall-outs on our homes keeping in mind their; i.e. Homes'; purity, security, stability and amicability at large. We shall go through the classified explanations and observations one by one.

With the supposedly peccant and aberrant people living right amongst us, we can only see and observe the human as well as moral values and principles to be violated and terminated for the fulfillment of their mean and foul ambitions. In fact this kind of attitude, perhaps, dominates us. What else can then happen on the earth or high up in the sky than the whole atmosphere becoming waspish and rancorous. To add fuel to the fire the lethal AIDS, apart from so many other problems or diseases, has broken out. The overall surroundings around us here have been receiving a complete change either because of the deliberate attempts on Nature or the irascible disposition towards the similitude Creatures. The deadly disease AIDS has been engulfing more and more areas or spheres with the people already having got poisoned with its virus resulting in the overall debasement and destruction of the whole human set-up. Every year we observe December 10 as the **"World AIDS Day"**.

In stead of communicating ideas, programmes and measures to combat and preclude it from permeating through our homes and societies, what we perhaps did and are still doing is that we are communicating this deadly disease through our bodies to more and more persons and areas only to lead us to the dead end street where-after the word "RESCUE" is unapproachable. This is corroborated by the fact that in the setting seventies there were no hazardous or worrying wrinkles upon our faces as there was no such disease. But in less than 15-20 years or so it has over-stretched its arm beyond control to more and more persons and regions. Our Scientists and Doctors have not yet been able to find out any congruous and effective medicine, so as to be equipped with, which could contain or do away with it. If we sincerely want this problem to be wiped out then we must warrant ourselves to the practice of self-containment and then let everyone have elbowroom to do his/her worth to blot this unprecedented hubbub out.

For this we must keep our homes insurmountable and inaccessible to it. But first there is a need to keeping the painful practice of Divorce out of our doorway to have a mutual understanding among the dwellers of our homes. We should discuss right here one more fact as to what kind of attitude our brothers and sisters have been maintaining in the context of this already hellish situation caused by this deadly disease. In stead of amending themselves, their deeds and attitudes, they are just busy in proving each other responsible for this hell and thus having yet another virus with them i.e. "Blaming-each-other" syndrome.

Let us just imagine the relationship between our brothers and sisters in which they are crossly entangled! Brother of a Sister wander about here and there to entice away the Sister of another Brother. Success in this kind of contemptuous craves is nothing as to what the answer to the question, what feedback they, i.e. our Brothers, gain in return, speaks. Nothing but only that their character is lost or assassinated and their mind, body and soul are defiled. And now the other side of the story is like this. Sister of a Brother roams about here and there to net in the Brother of another Sister. And what feedback our Sisters gain in return? Nothing except that they find themselves seduced, they are deprived of their chastity and thus their mind, body and soul are defiled.

Thus in both the cases we are de-sanctified by mind, body and soul and hence at a great loss which, in turn, is having a cumulative putrefying effect on our homes and societies. As a result we find both the affairs tried by us decalcifying and yet we long for such misdeeds as if we loved to be in the hellish situation. What remains the hope then for the upcoming generation when we are reducing our present homes to HOSPITALS? We need to amend our deeds and attitudes if we sincerely wish to clear this present diabolical atmosphere. Bearing in mind all these sentences the importance of the following saying receives a shot in the arm.

चारित्र्यं नरवृक्षस्य सुगंधि कुसुमं शुभम ।
आकर्षणं तथैवात्र लोकानां रञ्जनं महत ॥

i.e. **"Character is the most beautiful and consummately blossomed flower of ours being humans. Like a fully blossomed and enchanting flower the good and pleasing character attracts everybody towards one and pleases & impresses everyone who comes in contact with one."**

Our sole and pre-eminent duty is that we must not allow our homes to be used as an abode by the performers of such misdeeds so that they do not become abundant with carriers of AIDS virus. We ought to understand the importance that our homes must remain safe, strong and insurmountable by any kind of evils so that the situation thereafter can hardly have any source of ill-effects. Some other factors; like Drug Abusing and Pornography, are also contributing and supplying the necessary blood to this lethal disease AIDS by which it is encompassing more and more areas than what we cover through our insignificant essays in finding out some medicinal and psychological solutions. It is really a great pity that the kind of support that we badly need to fight this disease we are not able to get that; thanks only to our very known habits, playing pranks with none other than us. We shall try to discuss and put some torchlight into our essay of getting to know as to how Drug Abusing and Pornography play an inhuman role in bolstering AIDS and downplaying our efforts in fighting it out.

To be a drug addict proves of our having dangerous ceremonies. With our people fully sunk in the drugs and thus addicted to no good habit and culture what else can we expect of our future than to be destroyed and evaporated? Majority of our homes now a day is either aplenty with drugs or reserved and booked by their users. To add fuel to this hellish situation what we elders are doing might become crystal clear in the following few lines. It was a gentle February evening some 20-25 years ago when I was having an appointment with a Physician-cum-Cardiologist for my Grandfather suffering from some cardiac problems.

Here we shall have a vicarious gaze at the experience that I had had during a see-in with a 10-year old boy named "Kanishka" and his parents whom I met during my visit to that cardiologist. That cute little boy, too, had come along with his parents to have his father thoroughly tested and checked up if there was any serious cardiac disorder with him. I first introduced myself to them and then set out talking with that cute little boy. On being asked he told me that he was a student of class V and his father was a Civil Engineer.

During my chat with him I asked, "Your father is an Engineer; tell me what would you want to be in your life?"

He at once replied, "Engineer!"

I inquisitively once again asked, "Why?"

This time he whispered, "Money!"

I then pointedly inquired from him, "Now tell me honestly, what have you found conspicuous in your parents?"

On hearing this he paused for a moment but when I pressed upon him, he first fawningly eyed at his father and then reluctantly murmured, "Smoking and Drinking!"

Hearing this I was infinitely awestruck and his parents were having their heads hanging down, perhaps with shame. It seemed for a moment as if lest heaven should fall down. But the question that might crop up in anyone's mind is whether it was his faultfinding attitude towards his parents or had he wronged in calculating or reading his parents. The best thing that can be put forth for a 10-year young child is that he can only be simple, naive, pure and unsophisticated. He can easily have a crystal sketch of his parents by watching their sayings and doings and that answer was in confirmation of that very sketch.

A child can very well copy or follow its parents' activities as it happens of a child to be just like some water to adopt the shape of the vessel in which it is poured. That is why drugs have now found their ways even into our schools. What kind of future then do we have or hope of our offshoots and the next generation when we are nurturing them up in such a smothering air? This very attitude is rendering and condemning us to be frenzied and upset with the drugs having now found their abodes in our homes and schools. The dire need of the hour is the practice of persistent abhorrence from them if we really care even a fig for our future. We shall have to change or alter our attitudes if we elders wish to be respected, cared and loved by everybody, everywhere. As the age-old dictum speaks, **"Respect yourself and you will be respected."** The following saying confirms this statement.

# पदं हि सर्वत्र गुणैर्निधीयते ।

i.e. **"It is only virtues or values which make or let one have just and proper place and honour everywhere."**

The same kind of relationship is now needed with the drugs if we want or wish our offshoots to be not among the drug addicts. Drugs, in any way, must not be allowed to be carried into our homes or schools as they, in turn, will only vanquish them to the extent of no return. And thus if we do, indeed, have an eye or mind upon our children, teenagers, youths, homes, schools and society at large then we must not let out our homes to be used as an abode for storing drugs.

Now let us dwell upon the hot topic of Pornography. Can we have an open discussion on this? With the word "nudeness" perfectly abiding in our minds do we really need to be covered with clothes? Even though the known fact is that it defiles our very body structure, moral as well as physical, we have unceasingly been busy in benuding our sisters. How peccant and damn we have perhaps become, will be clear in the following few lines. Our respective mothers give us birth and do their best possible for our well upbringing. They do not spare anything or trifle away any moment in/for doing so. For this they do not display any kind of reluctance or hesitation on their part. The omniscient God luckily blesses us brothers with one, two or more sisters, too.

Then what an irony it seems that on one hand we happily live inside our homes with our sisters and mothers whereas on the other we ill-treat them by making or writing them nude outside our homes. With all this is the most surprising fact that we deliberately and knowingly show and write them de-clothed in our ill-intended exhibits, artifacts and writings. And after doing so we enjoy too as if some hidden treasure has been found or retraced. We show and write our those very sisters and mothers de-clothed in innumerable films, exhibits, stories and novels which our children, too, read and witness together with we elders. By doing or being involved in such mean and foul businesses what effect do we hope or expect on our next coming generation. What kind of foundation we have been erecting for them?

By doing so we only debase and corrupt our children, teenagers along with us and yet we hope to have models of good character. How can it be possible? Perhaps we are only to err as To err is human. But one thing is quite obvious that each one of us is now feeling guilty of one's own misdeeds because their after-effects have started playing havoc with and eating away our homes also. However, if we really and truly want to put this restive problem to a stand we shall have to be awake and start about restraining ourselves, together with others, from indulging in such ill-intended vice as it has now been touching on our raw. Better late than never! So we must set forth for the revival of our good senses as it has now been crossing the moral as well as human boundaries. In this respect the following lines help us a lot.

रवां प्रसूति चरित्रं च कुलमात्मानमेव च ।
रवं च धर्मं प्रयत्नेन जायां रक्षन्हि रक्षति ।।

i.e. " In the good and holy business of pro-tecting, maintaining and upkeeping one's woman or wife, which includes sisters and mothers also, one is deemed or sure to pro-tect, preserve, maintain and upkeep one's progeny, one's own character and one's self (dharma)."

Thus we must not let our homes to be used as an abode for storing or producing such ill-intended exhibits, artifacts or writing which defile and corrupt our children, teenagers and youths.

The BREATHLESSNESS session has buttressed us a lot in knowing fully well that our own homes provide for us the safest shelter and best succour whenever need arises, whether against natural calamities or manmade catastrophes. Exceptionally true is our conclusion because indeed our own home is the safest in-place that we crave to have at any cost. Our discussions in the Breathlessness session have also made several points of its importance and usefulness clear, which force us to rethink for its safety and stability. The responsible and worrisome labour of maintaining the same depends on the two exceptionally ornamental pillars called Wife and Husband. Being both dwellers and upkeepers at once it automatically becomes their duty not to allow their homes to be intruded into by the calamitous things so as to be doomed or drooped. Another fact is that our homes agglomerate into a society and in that very society we grow up and choose our life partners, i.e. Wife or Husband, to enter into a relationship of companionship.

From this point of view also we are bound to be actively working and purposely useful to our homes as well as society. We get our very first schooling, dream, think of and cherish our ambitions in our own homes. We are brought up and so trained in them as to befit the society well. In almost every moment, whether auspicious or opprobrious, we take refuge in our own homes. That kind of visionary home is the possibility if only the inhabitants or dwellers in a home are mutually loving, respecting and understanding. Only then the homes can be defined with the help of the words like safe, stable and concordant. Mutual love, respect and understanding are always the possibility if the dwellers, i.e. wife and husband, live in harmony, do have a taste for each other and take care of each other's interests.

Any wife and husband pair with this sort of exceptional relationship can provide everything needed or required for good upbringing of their offshoots so as to be self-dependent, disciplined and perfect in the future. This kind of visionary home is the outcome of only a sound and stable marital life with mutual understanding between and mutual love and respect for each other, i.e. wife and husband, or else thinking of this kind of homes will only be an imaginative contemplation. Sound and concordant marital life is the guest or invitee to sound marriage that is the outcome of hopeful good selection. With such an atmosphere inside our homes we can decidedly expect of keeping all the discussed ills out of our doorway to be HAPPY ADVIVUM[9].

Proverbs or sayings are important in our worldly life. They play a significant role in our worldly affairs. In fact, their presence alone approves of our having a behaviour in confirmation with the deeds and expectations of our worldly life and relationship. Each one of us might whole-heartedly agree with this opinion that without proverbs our domestic and social lives are incomplete. Not having any use of the proverbs in our daily life is just like a woman having no make-ups, jewels or ornaments on her.

As make-ups, jewelleries or ornaments play a significant role in a woman's life so

---

9    A state of Living with happiness.

also is the role of proverbs or sayings in our daily worldly life. The overall meaning is that proverbs are the make-ups and ornaments of our daily worldly life, family or social. The ensuing saying guides us to a great extent so as to have a safe, pure, concordant and harmonious atmosphere inside our homes.

सहृदयं सामनरयमविद्वेषं कृणोमि वः ।
अन्यो अन्यमभिहर्यत वत्सं जातमिवाध्न्या ।।

i.e. "O Dear house men and house women, there ought to be harmony, purity, concordance and understandingly good relationship in your family life and daily affairs. There ought to be no enmity and enviousness. Both you must make love with each other just as a cow cuddles, licks or makes love with its new born calf."

With the fearsome and deadly disease, i.e. AIDS, not finding its way into our homes we can hope of our offshoots to prosper and earn reputation and celebrity status to be one of the scholars, scientists, doctors, politicians, industrialists, musicians, philanthropists and many more such personalities with impressive character to be reckoned with in the years to come. Moreover each one of us longs for a mate, draws his/her sketches as per his/her liking and then set about looking for that fancy nob to be opted for the holy enchainment as it makes us learn to live befittingly in the society. Enchainment or Institutionalization is what we need and work for and in which we feel safe and perfect. Almost every achievement, easy or difficult, has been the outcome of pleasant and co-operative companionship, i.e. institution, wherein we are expected to work in a brotherly and friendly manner.

Without being institutionalized none bothers to care for and hence homes can be put forth as the perfect example of enchainment or institutionalization. This corroborates of a cyclic relationship in which we are bound to be sincerely and favourably active for the betterment of the atmosphere in and out of our homes. To be factually sincere everything, good or bad, helpful or hurtful, takes its birth and achieves its youth in our own closets. Hence it automatically becomes our duty to keep our closets guarded off from any kind of crudeness or roughness, whether natural or manmade. Mere thinking or contemplation will not do all but rather we badly need to set about and create an atmosphere to cash in on. And that atmosphere can be created only if we have co-operative mates with agreeable and concordant attitudes. This underlines the need for mutual love, respect and understanding between Wife and Husband.

In fact love for anyone begets in one respect for that person which helps to be on an understanding term with him/her. To be true and candid; to love is the invaluable and peerless, ought to be said noblest, quality inherent in and bestowed upon us by the omniscient God and to be loved is the invaluable and natural feedback one can hope to have from others. Love is the elixir of life which has been given gratis to us by the almighty and it alone has the capacity to cure all the maladies from which mankind often suffers. But it seems that we are little bit misguided today. What should have remained confined within the four walls has been locking us out of the same four walls!

What should have been a matter of respect

and comity has been proving a matter of disrespect and hostility! What should have been a source of inspiration and co-operation for all round development, natural as well as manual; is having been used as a source of exploitation resulting in the depreciation of all concerned values, moral as well as human! In fact Love is the root cause of every happening or incident, irrespective of its nature or content, that befall either on this earth or high up in the sky or down under the waters.

Out of love and affection for anything we are curious for that particular act or thing. We start manoeuvering, go on working endlessly and enthusiastically round the clock to end up with the fulfillment of that act or thing. Hence we can say that love plays the role of the precursor to everything and provides exact tutelage[10] to that ambition.

Whether it is an interpenetrating contemplation over any research or invention programme; whether it is an exemplification of how to make anything perfect and acceptable; whether it is a clandestine approach or meeting of the policy makers or industrialists

---

10   An act or process of serving as guardian or protector

to achieve something impossible; whether it is a purposeful exchange of ideas and views among the players of a certain game to win the match over; whether it is a long desire to see or meet the love-nob; whether it is a lovely proffer of wedding to the most affectionate person; whether it is a case of organizing or watching a tournament to be played; whether it is an exercising session of preparations for an examination; whether it is an elaborate attempt of picking and choosing a career and many more like jobs; in almost all the exertions love plays the role of the precursor and stimulates us to generate curiosity for that exertion due to which we plan and determine our future course of action. None of us can gainsay this fact. Even in writing this book love is playing the same role; i.e. the role of the precursor, in the name of humanity and goodwill.

Love for a thing begets in one curiosity which, in turn, begets desire for that thing. Desire gives birth to devotion that gives room for dedication and this, in turn, begets determination. Determination, to continue this unceasing series, gives place for labour that completes the series with the fulfillment of the ambition for almost every exertion. And thus it can be said that love plays host to everything that takes place inside or outside our homes. We can best explain the above series with the help of the following table.

LOVE
↓
CURIOSITY
↓
DESIRE
↓
DEVOTION
↓
DEDICATION
↓
DETERMINATION
↓
LABOUR
↓
FULFILLMENT OF THE AMBITION

Thus the main theme lies in the fact that due to love we, first of all, point our fingers at some aim and then set out to get and see that ambition fulfilled even if we encounter innumerable impediments. We just love to keep our spirit up to pursue our aim till we achieve that ambition. Quite often we are chopped in by the unknown impediments and sometimes amidst our ongoing operations we even receive injuries, physical as well as mental. In spite of all this we carry on until and unless we see the fulfillment of that ambition.

Hence arises the question that when we, at one hand, can be so friendly and obsequious to unnatural and non-living things how can we, on the other hand, be so inimical and inclement to our respective life partners who are natural as well as living that we opt for disunion with them, that we are not able to have an understanding with them. That we tend to have no love and respect for them in spite of the fact that they, too, are human beings like us. Isn't it an injustice and sin then in the name of humanity and almighty?

Of course, it is a vice and disrespect in the name of humanity and almighty. We willingly opt for living together with them in our closets and then hating or committing violence with them is the most unjust and sinful act in the name of humanity and almighty. So much so our good many forefathers taught us through their words and deeds to live amicably and harmoniously with others. Accordingly they wished to communicate, with our help, about the utmost importance of love and its loveliness, of harmony and its harmoniousness to our descendents. Presently it seems we are becoming more and more illusioned than illuminated.

Our children, teenagers and youths are the hopes and masters of the future and only a good and amicable home with mutually loving, respecting and understanding pairs of life partners can produce such recognizable masters in various distinguished faculties in the future. It is our utmost duty that we mould and educate our children and teenagers so as to be our hopes in future.

Anything can be made upright and good during its foundation or initial stages. Bearing this in mind we elders can be of much help and can provide measured guidance to them such as to be our masters in future. Along with them we, too, ought to amend and correct our conduct and mode of expression and only then we can expect a transformation or metamorphosis to take place. Children in the world are just like the fragrant flowers in the garden. And children in our homes are just like the blossomed flowers in the bouquet.

As we place suitably and decoratively our bouquets embellished with the fragrant flowers and then protect and preserve them with utmost care and sincerity to last more than expected or stipulated. The more salubrious and livable is the bouquet, the longer and better are the flowers kept, preserved and decorated. Exactly same is the story with our children too. The more salubrious and savoury will be our homes, the stronger and better can our children be brought up. Salubrious and savoury homes are the possibility only in case of cordial and wholesome relationship between the wife and husband pair.

A cordial pair can provide everything desirable, and in most cases needed to the child, for a healthy and sinewy upbringing. We must preserve them for the welfare and good cause of the mankind because they will be our workers in various fields and faculties in future across the globe. Whatever a child learns in its childhood that takes the shape of its basic knowledge, which in the later years blossoms out and guides it to behave accordingly. That is why homes are called the first and foremost schools for each one of us.

The better organized and inventive is the basic knowledge received by a child, the better it will confirm our hope that the child will be amply confident, intelligent and understanding in respect of the surroundings around it. From any point of view the conclusion is that our sole, sublime and utmost duty is to keep our respective homes safe and nutritious enough to be healthy and unconquerable.

This is possible only if it is occupied by a mutually loving, respecting and understanding wife and husband pair. Despite having so badly upset and tribulated what are we all doing now-a-days with our respective homes? Acting favourably or unfavourably? For their amelioration or deterioration? The best cumulative answer to all these questions that can be put forth is that we are, perhaps, unable to say anything.

Reason is that none wants to be humiliated either by the compelling circumstances or by others. Whereas today's genuine fact is that we are humiliating all but ourselves by indulging in several despicable deeds. To add to this unwelcome atmosphere come the painful practice of divorce wherein we dis-unite with our respective life partners fanning the ill-sense of separatism. This too has been causing a great deal of grim to the whole very set-up around us.

Considering and comparing all these ill-affecting factors and the present surroundings comes the outcome which speaks that we are, perhaps, no longer happy and peaceful and are irrefutably fed up with the whole lot of things and circumstances that are around us. This kind of whole lot has been giving rise to countless infirmities including those we have been discussing in this book. To add to this distressing atmosphere we have been mutely following the painful beaten track of divorce i.e. marry-go-tarry-go-empty. And that too in spite of the fact that we ourselves pick and choose our respective life-partners i.e. wife or husband and then embrace him or her with avowing before the Almighty that we will/shall be interwoven till our last breathe.

With this painful service on, the rationally constructed wholesome structure of our homes and society is being mystified and ac-erbated. We are just going on breaking down our homes and reducing them to the state of sordid nothingness for no good reasons and putting the lives of our progenies, together with ourselves, in jeopardy where-after we all can hope only to be destroyed or else at least polluted and direction-less. Thus, at one hand we are recurrently breaking down our homes here on the earth whereas at the other hand we plan to establish new homes in space and that too, with the hope that our foundation out there will be strong enough to withstand all kinds of outside pressure. What a paradox! The painful practice of divorce here has been eating away our mind, our bodies, our souls, our homes and our societies and thus has been staining our faces with countless unavoidable dark spots like the ills being discussed.

Therefore, instead of divorcing our own respective life partners, i.e. wife or husband, with whom we once erect and solidify our homes, shouldn't we at once think of divorc-ing the painful, venomous and very practice of Divorce itself? The need of the hour speaks in "YES" as there have been so many evils and/or ills embedded into our homes that they need to be effaced. With divorce firmly abiding in our society we are bound to be in this chaotic and problematic situation.

Moreover, we are in no ways better than the beasts who, for no fault of their own, just don't know the meaning of the sacred cord. There is no mutual rapprochement and understanding between them, there is no well-managed organization or institution among them and the result of not having such important and significant things is all quite clear. Many of them, i.e. their species, are either lost or facing the grave danger of extinction. They are not in a position of solving their problems on their own, they can neither provide any kind of sentimental or emotional security to each other, nor can they provide any kind of safety, security and stability in respect of their existence to each other.

Bearing all the above mentioned propositions in our mind let us have a comparative study between the modern and developed countries on one side and the underdeveloped and still developing countries on the other. In the modern and developed countries the world over it seems as if we wed or marry each other only to be divorced whereas in the underdeveloped and still developing countries this painful practice has started gaining in its ground and hence can be said that it has been creeping into the society. The most interesting and startling fact is that in spite of being educated and civilized, as we call, our people in the modern and developed countries opt for disunion.

In the modern and developed countries our boys and girls, before jumping to their final decision of marrying each other, experiment with and testify each other by being together as and under a qualified engagement for a stipulated span of time and yet in these very countries the number of divorced people is more than that of other countries across the world. With this the question that might sprout up in mind is that why this kind of strangeness prevails in our society. Why we, after our marriage, roll up our sleeves to divorce and/or to be divorced in those very countries? We must allow ourselves right now to construe about this fact bearing in mind the circumstances around us so as to chuck the painful practice of divorce away if we are indeed interested in making our homes and societies washed off all the evils and/or ills which have been having debilitating and devastating effects on our homes as well as our surroundings.

Being an Indian, what I can perhaps best do is that I shall let you all have a discussion right here on the conspicuous facts about Indian wedding customs and rituals and marital life as to why here the marital cord is considered honourable and thus paramount and unparalleled in the human world. We shall consider them one after another point-wise. The first and the most important fact is that here the social structure, internal as well as external, is such that the parents of the girls and boys try to settle the marriage of their respective nubile nobs which is as sweet as honey. The second fact is that here girls and boys are allowed to marry even in the case of their own choice, only when they get the wholehearted approval of their respective parents. The third fact is that here boys and girls are allowed or wish to see or meet each other before their wedding ceremony always keeping in mind each other's respect and dignity. The fourth fact is that here when one divorces one's life-partner i.e. wife or husband, or gets divorced one is automatically reduced to the sordid state of oneness and thus frozen out as the social structure, internal as well as external, emphasizes too much on couples than individuals. The fifth fact is that here the decision of marriage is considered personal as well as social matter and/or re-lationship due to which after getting married the couple becomes socially bonded also as corroborates the social structure.

As we know fully well the social alliance takes us after the responsibility of sharing and/or exchanging the illustrious idea of fraternity and brotherhood to more and more people and areas. So much so, it needs individual workmanship to be so to carry out this noble idea of strengthening the cord of social asso-ciation. And exclusive individual workmanship is a probability only in case of a decorated home with a co-ordinate enchainment of a mutually understanding wife and husband pair and those homes are the mute depo-nents of the genial atmosphere.

With this kind of homes and society as being discussed we can hopefully expect to have future quaint and exceptions. This kind of social association teaches our young couple to follow and emulate the long established holy traditions of doing something good and lucrative to the society by keeping their own homes impermeable to any kind of evils and/or ills as the sufferers of their side effects shall include our children too. Moreover, that kind of exceptional social association teaches and guides our couples to be busy in good deeds and not to be ostracized by their own wrong doings.

To continue the discussion about Indian social structure, internal as well as external, the another fact that calls for a place here is that to most of us Indians, divorce is a meaningless word like that somewhere occultly placed in the dictionary. It is a practice, which, to most of us Indians, is nearly equal to the impossible practice of plucking off a star from high up in the sky. But for the last some years, the painful practice of divorcing one's life-partner, once an unapproachable target, has speedily been gaining in its ground in the Indian society, too, and thus has become a catchword as the only solution to the marital unhappiness.

This kind of damn attitude together with

this painful practice needs to be nipped in its bud as we have been hopelessly observing its bad effects in those countries where it has become a household stuff. The painful practice of divorce and to some extent even an evil practice is causing us, together with our homes, to be burned away. We are socially emotional animals and such living beings don't separate or disunite but rather love to be harmoniously and agreeably joined with their respective partners. As we are fully aware with the philosophy that Man is a socially emotional being; who does not love to live in a society is either a devil or a deity. We are neither of them.

Besides we are obliged under **obligation of residence** to jointly live up to keep all the evils at bay. Hence we come to know that with this painful practice on, we can have its side-effects full of devilous nature which are quite unfit for our well being. After musing properly over the importance of good and amicable marital life inside the fragrant homes we have the outcome that divorce is not only a distressing factor but also a destroying one. One more fact that needs to be outlined here is that the more modern, educated and civilized we become in our appearance and countenance the more apathetic and insensitive we become in our attitudes as if stone age.

Do modernization, education and civilization then send one's senses of perception and good nature into oblivion? Do modernization, education and civilization make one egoistic and cynical in approach and by nature? If, however, such are the after-effects of modernization, education and civilization then each one of us will perhaps hesitate or show one's unwillingness from becoming modernized, educated and civilized. So we have got to invigorate ourselves with good human senses and then we should drown ourselves in the holy pond of humanity so as to be humane and compassionate.

Rightly and honestly assists the following quotation that "No one can justly censure or condemn another because indeed no one truly knows another". In simple words to be easily understood this enunciation is quite perfect as without knowing fully well others how can we explain anything about them and hence we can not just ill-speak about others. If, however, we do so we only expose our weaknesses in the sense that we are in-human and uncompassionate at once. Our homes, whether big or small, are our castles for us that provide us safety, security, happiness and peacefulness. A good home to have all these qualities is an expectation only in case of a good and wholesome marital life as the following two lines help us clear our doubts;

भार्यावंतः प्रमोदंते भार्यावंतः क्रियांविताः ।।

i.e. **"Men having ladies, i.e. wives, are always happy, joyous and blissful and those very men, i.e. a man having a wife, are wishfully and purposefully active".**

The second statement may be termed as its complement;

हता नीरसनाथा स्त्री हताऽसंरकारिणी च धीः ।।

i.e. **" The lady or the woman, whose husband is void of love, prosaic and insipid, ought to be considered as lost and dead in the sense**

**of completion of her desires. Just as the man
whose wisdom, prudence and witticism are
not with him is considered lost and dead".**

Bearing in mind above-mentioned propositions only stable homes with concordant and
understanding wife and husband pair can
discreetly act for the betterment of the overall
surroundings. Can you allow me to involve you
all in a brief and calculated discussion over
the family and social set-up we had had a
few years ago?

A few years ago when our joint or united
families were breaking into single or nuclear
families one after another it fell upon us that
we will suffer huge and irrecoverable loss out
of it. We felt all the commotion, hue and cry
over it. But when the breaking up of our joint
families caught up its speed and picked up
momentum we went limitlessly worried about
it. Even when our worrying situation could not
apply any brakes in the way to check this up-
trend, our single families started breaking up
with the help of the practice of Divorce.

Today we are in a fix over the increase in
the numbers of divorce and divorcees. This

present scenario is condemning us to feel the measurable share of these people who are throwing up totally new and unknown world of affairs. As we were helpless in controlling the rise in the joint families' break-up, we are much more helpless in containing single families' break-up. What are the reasons then that we are not able to contain or arrest the up-trend of our joint or single family break-up?

Several reasons such as unemployment, inflation, population-increase, settlement at far away places etc. may be cited as the helpers behind the rise. But happening of such incidents corroborates the fact that not only we have become self-centered but also that we have gone amoral and deviant. After the break-up of our single families what do we hope to be breaking? And what sort of society will be welcoming us?

The present circumstances compel us to read between the lines to put at risk every-thing in order to arrest the rise of single families being broken up. And homes with concordant wife and husband pair is a case just like killing two birds with one stone. We shall see that conspicuously.

Those homes can be an impervious abode to all the evils of animal life and we can expect our children to be among the celebrated people in the future. Besides by being so we, i.e. wives and husbands, can keep our homes unapproachable abodes to the evil practice of Divorce which can efficiently keep at bay the deadly AIDS.

It is only with this kind of exclusive homes we are slated to prosper or else we can only expect of our future, along with the present, to be hanging in balance feeling the lack of the concordant and agreeable atmosphere inside our homes and clear so outside. Our children, teenagers and youths all would restrain themselves from indulging in inhuman activities and becoming drug addicts. The other things that will help restore the inhabitants of our homes to normalcy and tranquility are mutual love, mutual respect and mutual understanding between each other.

Love and respect for other human beings and their emotions & sentiments could in no way infuriate the inhabitants of the homes to enable them to do something wrong, harmful and injurious which might later affect themselves in return. Besides mutual love and mutual respect, the other thing important is mutual understanding which, if tarrying in our homes, can be of a lot of help and succour to our children, our teenagers and our youths so as to be submissive, prudent and confident. And being so will preclude them from becoming one of the malefactors and drug addicts.

Thus, we find out that these three genuine catchwords, i.e. mutual love, mutual respect and mutual understanding, can play direct, first hand and decisive role in expatriating the roots of Drug Abusing, Pornography and the deadly AIDS. One more fact is that mutual love, mutual respect and mutual understanding tarrying in our homes we are automatically gyved into under the obligation of residence and humanity which stand erect against us in our way and prevent us from violating and/or going beyond the boundaries, moral as well as human. These evils and/or ills will only pollute our minds, our bodies, our homes and our societies which, in turn, could play injuriously and scurrilously with our lives and lead us to nothing by tyrannizing and playing the devil with our rightful and just living standards and surroundings. Therefore with some deter-mined endearing and toilsome jostling of our shoulders we can expect to have clear and dapper homes with pure air to breathe in and clear surroundings to live in.

As rightly and justly quotes the interesting catchy quotation which Chanakya, the Guru (teacher) of Chandragupta Maurya, once the king and ruler of Patliputra (now called Patna, the capital of Bihar in India) had inscribed in his book titled "Artha Shastra" (a book on worldly relationship and the subject of Economics) that "Those homes are indeed and must justly and truly be treated as a heaven if their inhabitants, i.e. the whole of family, which includes wife and husband together with the off-shoots, include obedient and just children with mutually loving, mutually respecting and mutually understanding wife and husband."

Bearing in mind the present clinking-ness inside our homes his sagacious keepsake seems to be of immense importance and inspiration as each one of us longs for a happy and peaceful life. So much so the other catch-word is that any of us will not detest being in heaven if provided. Again with that kind of homes our children, teenagers or youths will never be prompted or persuaded either by the circumstantial or environmental facts to be malefactors, nor will they ever run after annihilating drugs.

And on the other hand, as a matter of course, the wives and/or husbands, too, shall be under obligation of residence to act for and provide fresh and fair environment to their own off-shoots to live in. Thus, if we really and justly want to be in a happy and prosperous proposition then we must henceforth set out to have such circumstances and environments that we know that Mutatis Mutandis[11] we can expect to have. The other commanding fact is that our own homes are the best place so far as safety, security, longevity and tranquility are concerned and therefore we must not let our homes to be such as to be rattled and plundered away by any of the evils and/or ills i.e. Drug Abusing, Pornography and the all-too-pernicious disease AIDS, being shared in this book.

---

11   Those things having been changed which were to be changed.

Thus, our sole and paramount duty is to keep our own respective homes totally invincible to these ill-affecting factors; is to have mutual love, mutual respect and mutual understanding between us, i.e. wife and husband; is to provide everything needed and required for the well and dignified upbringing of our own off-shoots if we indeed wish to be so and lastly, is to provide for our scions an agreeable and pleasant atmosphere so as to be prosperous in the future.

# Divorce

OVERALL message that we receive from the chapter "Home" is that the pair called wife and husband is the necessary and pre-eminent requirement to a safe, stable and concordant home. Its technical foundation depends fully upon their humane shoulders and it is their practicality and prudence which run the home smoothly, agreeably and perfectly. Before elaborating upon the reasons and consequences of the painful practice of divorce, i.e. marry-go-tarry-go-empty, we ought to have a reappraisal session of our own deeds, good or bad, and their result or consequences.

But before doing all these we need to pause for a moment and hammer out the answers to the questions like those written hereunder. Where we are now and how far have we reached by practicing such deeds or services? What we are doing is right or wrong? Whether we should go on following the establishing inhuman painful tradition of disuniting with our respective life partners? Whether the practice of divorcing one's own life partner is just and rightful act or an injustice to oneself and the God who has descended us to the earth purely to continue with our help the long established good and desired human traditions among the people.

These are the questions one must put forth to oneself before divorcing or deserting one's own life-partner, i.e. wife or husband, as humanity and morality do not teach us to err by endangering the very existence of our respective life-partners and the very concept of goodwill but rather it teaches us to uplift the living standards and surroundings by be-ing proactive, receptive and co-operative. In fact this is an act which totally deserves to be disappointed and detested as it brings with itself frustration, bitterness and restlessness in our homes as well as our society.

By deliberately carrying on with this painful practice we are doing nothing but promoting evil and venomous side effects. At one hand, we are endangering our sane stability, natural as well as artificial, by playing foul with the things and whole very set-up which we have been endowed with. And at the other hand we are not sparing any moment and even tormenting with the similar human creatures and just reducing everything to be in a state of redoubtable predicament only to be bemused.

Thus going on jeopardizing our very stability along with the long established traditions, cultures and the everlasting prepossessing nature what we expect to receive in result. Nothing except that if we go on uninterruptedly and willingly or unwillingly following these deleterious or detrimental practices and/or activities we could only hope to be diminished and evaporated to the dropping and drooping stages.

Treating forwardly and apathetically with these very people with whom we once share everything needful and required to live together is the most sinful exertion coupled with

the most direful consequences. Not only it her-
alds our inhuman and fiendish nature but also
corroborates that we are untrustworthy and
non-cooperative with others which is quite
of a suffocating and disappointing composi-
tion. How despicable it is that we disunite with
those very people whom we once pick and
choose to willingly live together and take vows
to be with in any kind of testifying moments,
however grave or serious.

For how long could we be able to go on
with this kind of labyrinthine and choking atmosphere? If any befitting and handy solution
is not found soon the very institution of marriage will itself be shackled in with the boisterous side-effects on the homes and society just
like we have incessantly been receiving one
after another for the past couple of decades
or so.

The pious practice of marriage, as we all
know fully well, is the most important and
significant of all the stoppages which each
one of us experiences in the whole span of
our life. In fact everyone's real countable
life starts with the marriage and those who
achieve success after that pious stoppage

are reckoned with as the successful person, whether man or woman.

The life after marriage is much more important than the life prior to marriage. Another important fact is that if we could not get along well and hand-in-hand with our own respective life partners, the only person who lives together with each one of us and that too after receiving our wholehearted YES and willingness then how can we expect that we shall be at concordance with others who, only to our annoyance, do not live with us. Does it not prove that we are non-cooperative, selfish, dangerously crude and imperfect all at once?

As we have already discussed earlier that we boast of our civilization of being too much modern and developed. Do the words development, modernization and civilization then mean that the life becomes more and more miserable and mismanaged, thinking and/or attitude becomes more and more narrowed and reduced to the roomy status or nature? Each one of us will instantly turn down this kind of meaningless society and surroundings wherein none has the requisite prudence, confidence, cogent and co-operative spirit to work for the betterment of the surroundings, inside as well as outside our homes. Our experience speaks that development and modernization are the sole result of institutionalization wherein we harmoniously, co-operatively and effectively work together to carry on the existing good developmental trends.

The work of upliftment continues in spite of innumerable offending impediments, which we meet with in our developmental pursuance. We are considered the instrumental carriers of that incessantly continuing or unceasing works of upliftment. We have been labouring till now as these carriers for the time immemorial and we unavoidably need this trend to be carried on, anyhow, as we are passing through a severe testifying moment.

Now let us share some spiritual facts that we know. Ever since the evolution of man and woman and their relationship, our celebrated ancestors have always, through their lives, carried the importance of harmony and uniformity in their marital life and relationship. To the best of their ability, they carried this hallowed tradition of Marriage only to expect from us that we also carry their so important a message, for the benefit of the whole of mankind, during these testifying moments as well.

They established a hallowed tradition that we have been following without any doubt or query. They did not separate or desert each other till they breathed their last nor did they violate, under any circumstances, the traditions established by themselves in entire span of their life. They tried to teach us a lesson so as to enable us to follow that hallowed tradition with utmost earnestness and patience. They vanished from this beautiful world only after preaching us the importance of the institution of marriage. They also taught that happy, peaceful and concordant marital life is the true success of one's life.

A successful marital relationship is hospitably and honourably benevolent to the stability and longevity of the whole of the mankind. Even today our culture speaks that we are made to be culminated to marry and live happily. Not that after marriage we should divorce and get divorced and live culpably in a sorry state of affairs.

Let me have the liberty of taking you to the stage where we will discuss about reasons behind ourselves being divorced by our respective life-partners who love us and long for our companionship too. Circumstantial snags and individual compulsions can best be resolved by the involved parties themselves. It depends upon the facts that how much practical by nature, prudent by mind, understanding by attitudes and handy by activities we are. To be like this we shall first have to forsake our attitude of working with the notorious habit of having a pretentious, prejudiced or jaundiced eye. We shall have to revive our good senses, both by mind and by body, before taking on this problematic situation.

Homespun problems or misunderstandings can be worked out without much shuffling but only if one's spouse is co-operative, understanding and anticipating. Before looking at other people to have help or succour or some words of sympathy it is our native and pre-eminent duty that we should be such as to be worth calling for some constructive services to share as part of our respective distinction. But it is basic reasons that play host to several problems, generate differences and effuse tension between the parties involved thereby making their life miserable beyond any redress or retreat. We shall go through all those probable basic reasons, one by one, that stir up the peaceful atmosphere inside as well as outside our homes and drive the concerned parties to an utterly culpable state beyond any redress.

❖ Diffidence between life-partners, i.e. wife and husband, is the biggest factor which acts underhand as well as behind hand and evaporates only after the culmination to divorce and hence it ought to be termed as the root cause of this painful practice. In fact, diffidence is a word and practice which is highly offensive and obnoxious to any kind of relationship natural as well as manual. This evil word pours venom in any kind of relationship. It provides or proffers room for the neighboring evil consequential factors to have their lots after which they constitutively play havoc with the system to which they are concerned. Diffidence makes for confusion and perplexity where after the parties involved start thrashing upon each other. It gives birth to a situation wherein we start disrespecting and belittling the worthiness of our respective life-partners, i.e. wife or husband, which, in turn, makes for detestation.

❖ Detestation stimulates and stirs one up to loathe one's own life-partner. The detestable practice of loathing is the cause of suspicion between the life-partners. Being suspicious of anything and/or anybody poisons one's mind, body and soul and thus provokes one to the evil and deplorable sense of wrongdoing. Suspicion spirit with others gives preference to the lack of mutual understanding.

❖ Lack of mutual understanding ensenses both the involved parties in conjugal relationship to show cold shoulder to and shrink away from each other, which is the worst unexpected outcome of a wedding. It drives one to show disrespect to one's life-partner and thus surfaces the lack of mutual respect.

❖ Lack of mutual respect makes for marital infidelity, which is quite obnoxious to conjugal happiness, peacefulness and stableness. These are the things which we dangerously wish to have at any cost in our post-nuptial relationship. Lack of mutual respect between any two parties, whatsoever, is the confirmation of the attitude that they no longer respect the hallowed traditions continuing for the countless centuries and thus is an orifice for infidelity. When we have no respect for the centuries' long hallowed traditions which are only for our goodness and stableness then to whom, we shall be fiddle and that too up to what an extent.

❖ Infidelity prompts the involved parties to commit violence with or kick at or thrash upon or quarrel with each other. Violence or kicking or thrashing or quarreling with our respective life-partners exposes our weakness in terms of handling with others. So much so, this kind of deplorable demeanor towards others, especially towards the life-partners, is an injustice to oneself because it confirms that one is either a beast or a brute. Moreover, the violent behaviour contaminates one's mind, body and soul.

❖ Contamination and defilement of the mind, body and soul helps one but only to be apathetic and insensitive towards others which, in turn, makes one envious and utterly selfish. How strange is the fact that at one hand we are selfish and yet we ask for and expect some kind of assistance or succor from others in times of misery and catastrophe! What else one can expect of oneself after getting contaminated and defiled by one's very identity and existence but only that one is reduced to one's drooping stages.

❖ Selfishness is root cause of being non-cooperative and egotistic with the circumstances and surroundings. Being selfish is the sublime tumultuous likelihood which has only a lacerating effect on one's belongings, whatsoever. Non-cooperation among the workers speaks of all-round depreciation and destruction in every sphere, natural as well as manual.

❖ The evil sense of non-cooperation hardens one's attitude and hence totally acerbates the whole atmosphere around one which, in turn, enrages one's mind and body to the devastating extent. Hardship and acerbation are the words totally inimical and calamitous to the very identity and existence of the mankind.

❖ Enragement of the mind and body promotes and sends one into a world where non-conscience and amorality lord it over others. Getting easily enraged by mind and body exposes one's weakness only in terms of witticism and wisdom. Enragement of the mind and body enfeebles one's thinking capability and working capacity and thus one is easily reduced to the doomsday.

❖ Enfeeblement in the thinking capability and working capacity devitalizes one's moral as well as intellectual characteristics and body strength. This kind of situation is quite a grievous one to the whole of the mankind as it not only plays truant with one's indigenous working capacity where after one is haplessly reduced to a situation of good for nothing. This is quite a disgruntling and discouraging situation as it causes deprecations in moral as well as human values and with it, i.e. enfeeblement, one is out of control and not oneself.

All these factors cumulatively act and play underhand an important role in formulating one's out-coming expressions and thoughts. Any single factor among the factors elaborated above paragraph-wise can infuriate and tea us up where after we become impassive and uncompassionate towards others whereby we are driven forcefully to divorce or disunite with our respective life-partners. Moreover, some conjugal relationships happen to be totally based upon sex and sexual intimacy, i.e. coition, and the fact is that we are not all flesh and blood.

Anyway, divorce, too, can be reckoned with as one of the concealed causative lending a helping hand in embittering the surroundings inside and outside the homes and societies the world over by giving birth to hazardous problems being discussed. These problems have been playing hide and seek with us with no concrete solution in sight as yet.

In spite of having full knowledge of these ill-effects of divorce we have been going on and on with this painful practice without having full technical knowledge of our own minds together with the homes and societies. It exposes our inhuman nature with frenzied state of mind and body. Thus, calculatedly divorce besides causing these discussed evils and/or ills brings with itself bitterness, frustration and restlessness to homes and societies.

As it breaks up our well erect and stabilized homes with wife and husband desolating each other leaving behind a non-dapper atmosphere wherein the offspring, whether children or teenagers and in some cases youths, too, oscillate like a pendulum between their parents only to feel unsafe and insecure, emotionally as well as physically, where after they can expect of themselves being easily pushed to their doomsday. The whole of the family is annihilated thereafter. For feeling and for viewing that kind of future i.e. uncertain future, awaiting them, i.e. the off springs, they make out in search of safety, peace and happiness where they find nothing to their rescue as their very own closets or homes are already collapsed.

They come only to know from others that their own closets or homes have already been demolished beyond repair or modification by none other than their own parents and henceforth no other person can provide any kind of asylum to them. It is this very point and situation where they, i.e. the offspring, find drugs as their only intimate and confidential recourse. Thereafter they start dragging themselves, which badly affects their mind, body and identity as humans. Owing to this unkind situation inside and outside our homes we have been receiving the augmentation in the number of drug addicts and hence have been finding this evil practice beyond control. Some, after getting discussed by their own relatives, are allured also by others to commit crimes and become male-factors. Both Pornography and AIDS are, in most cases, the outcome of our regularly divorced parents.

All these reasons have been condemning

us to properly muse over and over again to do something just and concrete as soon as possible as we know fully well that drugs have now found their ways even into our schools. Drugs must not, at any cost, be allowed to dominate our children, teenagers and youths along with our homes and societies. For this we shall have to solidify our homes well and then shall have to have a solidarity and understanding among the inhabitants, whether wife, husband, teenagers, children or youths. Divorce is caused by some other reasons also which need to be particularized here.

Mutual crushing down to each other's desires and interests, mutual prejudicial tendencies towards each others' attitudes and activities, mutual mal-treatment with each other etc. are the especial causes in giving birth to this painful practice. Resolving all these factors depends on the conscientious fact that how much practical, prudent and acknowledging one is. An impractical and incognizant person cannot only do nothing to help reanimate and stabilize the living atmosphere and surroundings around him/her but also that he/she can only help become vapid and beclouded in his/her own life together with his/her dependents.

As the great Chanakya, the Guru (teacher) of Chandragupta Maurya, once the ruler of Patliputra (now called Patna, the capital of Bihar in India) and the author of the very first book on Economics, put it, "It is most unfortunate, disappointing, suffocating and tedious for one if one serves and/or does one's good services to an impractical and non-acknowledgeable master who hardly knows about the happenings and the surroundings around himself/herself". With these lines fully embedded in each one of us, we should try to be a person practical and acknowledgeable of the happenings around.

To support it comes the quotation picked and chosen and then put forth right here. The quotation speaks that "A successful person cannot be reckoned with as the rightful, just and committed to the responsibilities but rather a virtuous man can easily be reckoned with as such and can easily have everything present around him/her needed for useful life". All in all we come to the conclusion that the utterly painful practice, to some extent an evil one too, of divorce has been proving one of the iniquitous factors that have been adding fuel to the fire in destroying our homes and society one after another.

This painful practice of divorce has also been the cause of the rampant problems like Drug Abusing, Pornography and AIDS. All these have been lording it over others for the last couple of decades or so and thus have been badly affecting and afflicting our peaceful and standardized living. Thus divorce stands erect against our developmental trend and spirit. Therefore, first and foremost, we have got to struggle for the removal of the evil spirit, as soon as possible, with which divorce is used as a weapon for materializing the conjugal differences if we really care for the sincere revival of the good senses in us as humans for the survival of the mankind as this painful practice is an injustice to we humans as well as the God.

# Marriage

AFTER finding or having knowledge of so many evils and/or ills as the outcomes of the painful practice of divorce, we shall now gird up our loins to have concrete and conclusive session about the reasonableness and usefulness of the reverential practice of marriage and marital life. Marriage is the practice revered and longed for whereas divorce is the practice odious and hated in almost every nook and corner across the world.

Marriage is the consummation of DESIRES, the fulfillment of NATURAL IMPULSES and is the CROWNING GLORY of one's life. Marriage not only means marital relations and compromise and understanding in sexual relations, it, on the other hand, implies union of minds and spirits.

Mind, body and soul in case of conjugal relations are blended in one harmonious whole. There is no jarring discordant and unhappy note in true marriage, for true marriage is the wedding of two souls or two minds that think together or two bodies that work together in complete and perfect unity and integrity or perhaps unison of two hearts that beat side by side in true harmony. No human being, whether man or woman, can lead a lonely, isolated and self-centered life. The sanctity of marriage can be realized in terms of true and concordant companionship.

Marriage is the fulfillment of God's plan that has been alive and continuing for countless centuries. But now-a-days, it seems, we have been too much involved and/or busy destroying our well-solidified homes. We are dangerously racing on the establishing beaten track of marry-go-tarry-go-empty with no proper heeding to its repercussions. The questions, which then might come or brew up in everyone's mind, are written here under. Have we become so impassive and selfish that we could no longer be compassionate towards others, particularly our life-partners?

Have we depreciated so much in moral as well as intellectual values that we no longer care for and/or pay any heed to the genuine demands made from and advises rendered to us? If the answers to these questions are in negative then all right but, if they are in affirmative then yet another question arises. For how long we could proceed or go on like this and what would be the ultimate outcome? In fact we are doing nothing but playing truant with ourselves.

In answer to all these questions let me report here an accidental encounter that I had almost 11-12 years back with a person named Dilip Rahi and his wife Sarla Rahi. They were hardly a two or three years old married couple. I came across them when they were having an appointment with my father, who was a lawyer by profession, and there I came to know that they were going through the final stages of the painful practice of divorce. They had their legal papers of divorce nearly prepared and all was about to end in next few days.

When I came to know all about that from their very mouths, I was naturally very much astounded with their opinions and final decision. They were just resolute to disunite with each other because of utter confusion and crankiness between them. On hearing this, I set about brooding of some idea so that this painful practice could be averted or avoided at any cost and the love spirit lost between them could be restored or retraced. Seeing and receiving their approval, I instantly offered one piece of paper with two drawn columns therein to each one of them. Then I separately talked to each one of them and asked to write down all the demerits which they both find in themselves and the merits, which they both observe in their partner respectively in the two prescribed columns.

After making such business they both handed over their respective folded papers back to me and then I, after receiving them, interchanged and crossly handed them over back to each one of them. When they were going through their respective papers I kept on glancing at them and in course found them complacent, revealing and chuckling. Since then 8-9 months passed by without any information. But fortunately one day when I came across them again I was extremely delighted to know that they were expecting to be parents in a few months to come and that they had divorced the very and deplorable idea of divorcing each other.

Thus, this incident confirms that marriage is a case of only mutual rapprochement, which is mostly needed and called for. It does take time to be in the absolute rapprochement but one ought to have patience and self-confidence. Another important fact is that any person, whether man or woman, gets only once in his/her whole life span the real and true partner and that is his/her own first and foremost wife/husband. After divorcing or getting divorced with that very first life-partner it is nothing but only playing vacant with oneself.

When one disunites with one's first ever real life-partner it becomes impossible for one to run with any other next partner in the same groove as one's mind and body are already wounded and injured and always susceptible to the first unstable conjugal relationship and unwanted and uncalled for disunion. Yet another important fact is that mutual differences between wife and husband will always exist because to differ is natural and is the illustrious symbol of a healthy relationship.

Husband and wife are like the two wheels of a carriage, the carriage does not move any more if any one of the wheels is faulty and imperfect. For the carriage to move smoothly and timely, the wheels must move in perfect accord. A husband and wife pair must live in peace, harmony, friendship and mutual love, mutual respect and mutual understanding. This kind of relationship is good, useful and suitable to our homes and society. Being complementary to one another comes the following and replete with the knowledge of the importance of this kind of exclusive relationship.

यः सदारः सः विश्वास्यः तस्माद दाराः परां गतिः ।।

i.e. "The man, having a lady (wife), happens to be dependable, accountable, trustworthy. Hence, woman, i.e. wife, is the most needed, important and significant achievement for a man. Having woman, as wife, is a matter of great pleasure and satisfaction for a man".

In any case womanless, ladyless, wifeless and familyless person or man invites a lot of suspicion before being depended or trusted. Now we shall go through the second aspect of the coin i.e. its complement.

नातंत्री विद्यते वीणा ना चक्रो विद्यते रथ: ।
नापति: सुखमद्येत या र्यादपि शतात्मजा ।।

i.e. **"Just as a lute or a lyre is useless, worthless and good-for-nothing sans its wires and as a chariot is half, semi-complete, forlorn, worthless and itself a burden without or sans its wheels, a lady or woman without having a husband is never happy, secure and peaceful, invites a lot of problems to her service, feels lonely, forlorn and depressed. It does not matter at all whether she has as many as hundred sons, many more, almost innumerable, relatives and friends and what not".**

Besides these two complementary sayings or dictums the following line provides us a just, proper and useful guidance, along with giving an introspective view of our homes, in order to have security, stability, integrity and longevity in our personal, family and social life.

न गृहं गृहमित्यादुर्गृहिणी गृहमुच्यते ।
गृहं हि गृहिणीहीनमरण्यसदृशं मतम ।।

**i.e. "Not only a home is called a home, but rather a housewife is called a complete perfect home. If there is no housewife in a home then it means, it confirms that the very home is a jungle, and assimilation of forest goods.**

This saying is indeed right and meaningful to its words. Truly and justly a housewife is defined, adorned with exclusive words according to the services with which she maintains or keeps up her house to a majestic. The better managed and dapper is the home the more confident, happy, satisfied, honorable and well educated means and looks its housewife. The whole maintenance and upkeep of a home is a matter totally related to its house wife and that is why a housewife is called a home and ought to be called so indeed.

Moreover, our offspring take pride and get

immense pleasure in their parents and such kind of homes and can then be an able and useful partner and supporter to the home and society in future. These kinds of homes are capable of keeping their inhabitants away from the harmful evils and/or ills i.e. drugs abusing, pornography and the deadly AIDS. Harmonious homes make a harmonious society wherein we can harmoniously grow up with our minds perfectly sound and our bodies perfectly supportive to us. But the strangest fact is that after we are successful in establishing an absolute understanding spirit and rapport with our respective life-partners we cater to disunion whereas on the other hand union is strength.

When we become perfectly corded and stringed we divorce our respective life-partner. Why does this kind of strange and outlandish attitude prevail among us as a result of which only harmfulness or hurtfulness can be expected? There is one more point behind this painful practice which, I think, we must discuss right here. The very word "Life-Partner" itself sounds little bit objectionable and contemptuous. There is a considerable need that we must stick to the calling of only wife or husband as the case may be.

To be candy and candid, partner in a class-room, business, outing, expedition, study, invention works or something temporary is, without any doubt, alright but in life and that too after getting enfettered in the holy, unbreakable and respectful cord of wedding, i.e. Marriage, in order to live as one in home for permanent till one's last breathe and who bears happily and patiently with us all kinds of moments, whether joyful or sorrowful, easy or tense.

It is indeed too bad, derogatory and dis-graceful one to call and treat our respective wives or husbands as mere partners. The call-ing of wife or husband itself sounds perfectly respectful for the respective personality. Hence we must immediately put off or aban-don calling our wives or husbands as mere life-partners. Now we shall have a discussion on the factors which sum us up to eventually jump to the final decision of dissolution and on how to tackle with them. All the factors have already been outlined paragraph-wise in the one-up chapter of this book.

When they, i.e. the factors, one after another add up and get crystallized we are, after that, dominated by the amassed thoughts in the mind and the only way out that rushes up to us is the painful practice of Divorce, the most coterminous step after that aggressive conglomeration. So we shall once again go paragraph-wise.

First, diffidence shows the other side, i.e. the negative aspect, of our behaviour, the imperfection and clumsiness of our mind and body. It eats away our mind and body and means that we are less confident of ourselves which must not be or else we shall unmanageably put us in danger at almost every step. It works as a high stimulant towards acerbating the whole set-up of our mind and body and has its only offensive side effects on our homes and societies. This must not be let onset our mind and body for our own stability, mental integrity and longevity. It stands erect against our own personal sound and sane development. Hence it must be flown away into the oblivion before it starts eating away us, our mind and body, our homes and society and doing so will need our wholehearted help, honest approach and mutual understanding terms among the inhabitants of homes, i.e. society.

Next come detestation and loathing. These corroborate the fact that we are bored and annoyed with no one else but ourselves and the whole set-up, individual as well as social, arranged by and around us. Boredom makes us lethargic and de-energized so as to be impediments to the all-round development of our mind and body. Thus, detestation and loathing are the words which themselves deserve to be detested and loathed at once.

To add to this chart come words like suspicion and lack of mutual understanding. Being suspicious of something and/or somebody and on mutual misunderstanding terms with others are the complexities which cavil at our very identity of being humans as we are acclimatized and accustomed to a co-operative, understanding, reconciliatory and seemingly pleasant living. With a suspect look and lack of mutual understanding we can not keep up well with our respective life-partners, i.e. wife or husband, whereas wife and husband are the backbone of our homes and hence the society. So much as to keep our own respective homes safe and sound we must not harbour any place for suspicion and mis-understanding. These are mostly needed with the co-sharers to be on the progressive spirit and stairs. And hence the onus of keeping the ceiling, i.e. the roof-top, safe and sound solely depends on the two ornamentally and invaluable pillars called wife and husband and that there must be no suspicion and mu-tual misunderstanding between them if such is indeed the objective.

Then, comes the word lack of mutual respect. Respecting others is the most out-standing and picturesque merit of a morally good behavior as well as a human being. We are taught and preached right from our birth to pay respect and honourably surren-der to others. But showing disrespect to our own life-partner in spite of them being similar creatures, picked and chosen by ourselves, is not a reputable dealing. In fact with perfect mutual understanding and/or mutual respect and/or mutual love we can desirably help ourselves develop to absolute consummation and sophistication of the mind, body and soul.

So, there must be a feeling of mutual hands-up respect in between life-partners, i.e. wife and husband.

Next befall the words infidelity and violence. Fidelity and non-violence are the two mostly needed and required terms in the post-nuptial relations. We consider the similar human creatures an invisible mirror representation, i.e. mirror image, of the almighty. We show our true and full fidelity to Him in times of sorrow or misery and joy or happiness. With this point and thinking inextricably harbouring in our minds we should not be disloyal to and/or at violence with our respective life-partners in the closets. But what on earth has made us so rude and crude that we just avoid knowing anything about the fact that we are only misleading ourselves to our doomsday. If we indeed wish to continue with and have any love and respect for the God's plan then we must restrain ourselves from demeanouring like this or else we shall be on the decaying path. And violence with the life-partners means that we do not at all believe in humanity as it teaches us to have respect for and be co-operative towards others.

The most dependable pillar for conjugal harmony, happiness and success is that we must have allegiance to our respective life-partners. What has been misleading and causing us to err despite all the constant warnings is nothing else but the fact that our mind, body and soul are perhaps no longer pure. That is why we have been observing a slow but steady alteration in our modus ope-randi[12] as well as modus vivendi[13] which are the mootpoints of today. In fact, the very word contamination itself sounds contaminated.

Now we shall alight at some other facts weighty enough to be given a place here. All of us love children because of their having simple naturalness and unsophistication. But, that loving simple naturalness and unsophis-tication have been disappearing because of our children, along with teenagers and youths, having more and more indulged in drug abusing and crimes. So much so that our once guiding elders now-a-days, instead of correcting our children, teenagers and youths, themselves indulge in the blasphemous

---

12  The term is used to describe someone's <u>habits</u> or manner of working, their method of operating or functioning.

13  A manner of living; a way of life.

activities like pornography and the AIDS and thus have been falling prey to these evils and/or ills.

Being so what can one expect to be? Nothing else, but defiled and contaminated. We have been observing their hurtful effects on our homes and society. That is why we are becoming more and more contaminated. Hence there is a pretty dire need for a change in our modus operandi as well as modus vivendi for the goodness and welfare of our homes and society. If we indeed want to be out of all the evils and/or ills being discussed in this book we shall have to make ourselves as well as the present surroundings agreeable and accommodable.

Then we shall have to correct our own homes with the inhabitants, particularly the elders because children and the upcoming generation will be following them in their pursuance, whether good or bad. And then that cycle will end only with our making the surroundings agreeable to us as homes provide an integral shelter for us. The only seemingly way out is that we must avoid being enticed or allured away and be deliberated to use drugs, to be malefactors, to be pornographic and to be an AIDS virus carrier.

For all this we must have an agreeable and concordant atmosphere inside and outside our homes so that our children, teenagers and youths are not amongst the defiled and contaminated in order to be prospering in the future. Similarly we elders must not violate the rule of the sane and pious homes as they demand and demonstrate an agreeable and harmonious wife and husband pair to be helpful to making the homes and societies clear off any kind of defilement and contamination, whether by mind, body or by soul. Homes, as we all know full well, constitute a society and a country totally depends on its people dwelling in that homes and society. Thus, it proves that for a healthy and developing country, its people must not be defiled and contaminated so as not to be the impediments in its all-round developmental track.

To continue the table come words like selfishness and non-cooperation. It is quite a no denying irony that in spite of the fact that we live in homes and society with the similar creatures and always long for to be in companionship with others we are selfish and non-cooperative and yet we hope to prosper. Development of our mind and body depends purely on the feeling of co-operation and unselfishness. Moreover, to allay all the evils and/or ills from our homes and societies we need to be co-operative, unselfish and rational. So is the reason that we find no selfish and non-cooperative person fully developed and consummate by his/her mind and body. And with mind and body unripe and tremulous we can only expect to be accursed by others including the Almighty. Thus, to be on an intimacy and reciprocal understanding with our respective life-partners we need to be unselfish and co-operative.

To complete the table come words like enragement and enfeeblement. Riding the sense of selfishness makes one enraged and being on non-cooperative terms with others makes one enfeebled by mind and body along with the collective physical strength. This is a fixing situation which misleads us to disunite with our respective life-partners instead of keeping up well and going hand in hand with them. Enraged and enfeebled homes and societies must immediately be demolished before they could affect other sane and sound homes as the inhabitants in those kind of vociferous houses are neither supportive to the mankind nor they are helpful to themselves, being weakened by mind, body and their collective physical strength.

Thus, all bad and offensive start with the censorious and condemnable diffidence between the two ornamental pillars of a home, i.e. wife and husband. If we are to correct and make our homes clear and pure, we shall have to be cautious and always reformative about our own deeds. We shall have to be at distance from all the social evils being discussed. Today instead of doing so, we use our energy only in censoring and condemning each other for our mutual acrimonious deeds only to add one more feather to this already hazardous and hellish surroundings. We have been putrifying our surroundings by our officious attitudes towards climate as well as similitude creatures, which must be distasted and disallowed.

So, when we could not do any justice to ourselves how could we do any justice to others by censoring or condemning them? Have we got any right or authority for doing so? Perhaps the following few lines put everything to order when the quotation is picked and chosen and written hereunder. Each one of us is unique and thus totally new and unmixed with. When we do not know full well about ourselves in respect of nature and attitudes, how can we then certify anything about others in same respect, condemn or censure others.

Condemning or censuring others will prove of us being uncivilized and faultfinders which is not commendable from any measure. And it is dead certain that most of us will wholeheartedly agree with this quotation. Moreover, so far as we humans are concerned we have not been descended by the Almighty on this magnificent earth to censure or condemn each other but rather we have been descended to extol or encourage each other to make the surroundings and the nature around us agreeable and cooperative as we presume that the omnipresent God is present in we humans also. But despite this very fact we censure, make violence and disunite with our respective life-partners and yet we wish to be happy whereas true happiness resides in good companionship of mutually loving and respecting people.

One thing that needs to be discussed right here is that we first pick and choose suitable persons and then go through the thoughtful test-each-other session before finally jumping to the holy and cherished decision of wedding. Even then the most outlandish fact is that we disunite, we divorce our respective life-partners and that too, after becoming well acquainted with each other. This not only confirms that we ourselves are imperfect but also that we do not have full confidence upon us. Therefore, first of all, we must be perfect and confident of ourselves.

One more thing that needs to be outlined right here is that any person, whether man or woman, can have only one true and loyal friend in his/her lifetime and that friend is his/her very first life-partner, i.e. wife or husband, with whom he/she can run in the same groove after having some mutatis mutandis i.e. some mutual circumstantial accommodation. Mutual circumstantial accommodation here means care for each other's desires and interests.

When we first disunite and then remarry with some other person, that is only a formality to be traditionally processional and at concordance with the society. At this very point, one's ego and countenance are most hurt and humiliated.

What could have been done without any harm or loss in the very first alliance, i.e. Marriage, we do all those things in the second alliance with too much eagerness, but harm and insult to ourselves. That is why when one disunites with one's own first life-partner, one is never happy thereafter, whether alone or remarried, because one is already defiled and embittered with the failure in keeping up well with the very first life-partner.

One's self conceit is perhaps hurt most when one remarries, reunites with somebody else as one fully knows that one has already been divorced and/or deserted by one's first life-partner and that there must have been something wrong with oneself. So, instead of following the panic-stricken tradition of divorce and re-marriage we should amend ourselves so as to be loved and revered by our own respective life-partners.

Thus all these factors call for true adherence to one's first ever life-partner or else the surroundings along with the living will become more frustrating and venomous as has been for the last few years or so.

To support this claim, i.e true adherence to one's own life-partner, comes another statement that in order to have a good and amicable relationship and companionship with the life-partner, i.e. wife or husband, some amount of difference in the thinking as well as working attitude are bound to arise or take place, but they all need endurance and patience from us to be solved out.

At one hand when we put aside each and every impediment or problem that comes in our way in our prospering and upkeeping exercises or works and continue pursuing our aims to ultimately get success why then at the other hand we do not keep up well with our respective life-partners despite the fact that we ourselves pick and choose them to have a companionship and relationship with. If we can not keep up well with the sole life partner, i.e. wife or husband, if we do not have any joyful and peaceful relationship with the sole true companion then from any point of view divorce is not the only solution as we, after getting divorced, then start longing for another companion and this trend continues till we are totally defiled and contaminated.

So much so, another high and true fact is that marriage is a holy and inviolable institution on the face of religion as well as social customs and bindings. And hence the sanctity and dignity of the holy institution of marriage must not be disgraced, violated or neglected at any cost and under any circumstances.

Therefore, from every point of view we arrive at the conclusion that we must stick to our only spouse and avoid divorce so far as possible for good upkeep of the offspring; for good intimated and fragrant air within the four walls; for good and agreeable working atmosphere outside the four walls; for purging the air off the evils and/or ills that are dangerously pressing or bearing down upon our minds and bodies and above all, for maintaining and augmenting the sanctity and dignity of the holy wedding cord so that the generations to come must have a respectful and immutable look and attitude toward it and they must follow this holy custom unquestioningly always bearing in mind its very sanctity, dignity and celebrity.

With this kind of good and high thinking attitude always dwelling in our minds we can hopefully expect promising future for our offspring together with us. It is high time to awake and get busy in doing so if we care, even a fig, for our homes and society and the future, which always awaits us.

# Decision Points

"Be the change you want to see in the World".

(Mahatma Gandhi)

NOW we shall fall onto the most important part or topic of this book. Men and Women have been descended on this magnificent earth by the Almighty to harmoniously continue the perennial cycle of identifiable and incontestable existence of the naturally magnificent world continuing for the countless centuries. The Almighty carries out his wishes through us, whether for improvement or droopment.

    This beautiful and prepossessing world welcomes everyone with utmost salutations, allocates everyone enough space to have an abode throughout his/her life and sadly bids goodbye to its people when their end looks imminent. Thus, we are only the passengers of this perennial cycle.

What are the duties then of us being passengers? Whether to make that cycle dirty, blemishful and jammed enough to be ruffled, deplored and disgraceful or to maintain that cycle honourably pure and clean enough to be unquestionably pursued? The true and uncontestable fact is that none loves to be calumniated or humiliated, even for his/her own faults and failures.

So when we, at one hand, do not love to be treated as such then why do we, at the other hand, want ourselves or send invites to be accursed and reproved for our deplorable activities and attitudes by our scions when vanished from this world? This is indeed a touchy question that should be put forth before each one of us and then should be allowed to play on our own respective roles being human beings.

One thing which is crystal clear is that this worship able world bewails bitterly at those who work for its all-round betterment, well upkeep and standardized stability when they breathe their last and does not care for or ask anything about those who do not shed even a drop of blood for its being so. One can have a wild guess about those as to what kind of treatment they deserve when they work only for its decay and destruction.

It pays its high tributes to its upholders and well wishers. There were and are countless such personalities around us. But the main thing is that the omniscient God has blessed every person, whether man or woman, with one remarkable merit. That remarkable merit is the ability to amend our activities and attitudes. If there is resoluteness in our will power then we can have a definite and graceful change or alteration in ourselves, our attitudes as well as activities. Each one of us can be a useful asset to his/her family and society by amending himself/herself.

The present hour calls for the good and purposeful use of that remarkable merit right now. What we men are today losing is nothing but most precious indigenous character. Any person, whether man or woman, is defined by his/her own character. A lose in character is considered to be the greatest loss in one's life i.e. character lost means everything lost.

Each one of us receives insult or respect in one's family or society according as his/her character demands or deserves. Character is everything for each one of us. As we all know full well that good health is above wealth. That is why when we get indisposed or a fall in our health we do spare nothing, neither any money nor any moment, so as to be recovering to gain our previous original good health. And good health is an invitee or ultimate guest to a good character.

Absolutely correct it is because we men, in any case, must not lose our character as the family, home and society all love us because of our worthiness and worthiness, as we know full well, lies in our own character. The assiduous onus of keeping one's health good and salubrious purely rests with the good and spotless character. See the below Table.

**SPOTLESS CONDUCT**

↓

**RIGHTEOUSNESS**

↓

**TRUTH**

↓

**GOOD DEEDS**

↓

**SELF-POWER**

↓

**PROSPERITY**

And after going through these lines who would not want to be prosperous? Almost everyone would! Which creatures on the earth do not have the full technical meaning of all the six catchwords? All but we humans do not have and yet we ourselves have been behaving like others as if something fiendish or beast like. Thus we come to the point that character must anyhow be preserved and upheld and that is lucrative and rewarding, too, for us humans.

Similarly modesty and purity are called the women. Everywhere in the world women are loved and revered because of their modesty and purity. Most of the women might also agree with this concept. But are they falling in line with this conception and doing worth their calling? The onus of sincerely answering this question should be left to them. Women are our sisters and relations and hence they should be treated keeping in view the kind of relationship. We men, too, should provide elbowroom for them to be working freely, constructively and productively.

Today, at one hand, we men are losing and debasing our own character, whereas on the other hand, we women are losing and putrifying our own modesty and purity. Again let us contemplate over another reality which is of too much importance and needs to be discussed right here. Children of any sex are cradled and fondled all over the world. Why?

Because of their possessing simple natural-ness, naivete, unsophistication, purity, straight-forwardness and truthfulness and what not. The list is simply endless. We find or observe in them everything; i.e. modesty, purity, spotless character, immaculateness, obedience, cal-culated inquisitiveness, familiarity and many more such characteristics. That is why they are considered inherent mirror representation of the omnipresent God.

To be true and candid, exactly the same is the case with us. If only we men could save our character from getting assassinated by anything offensive and hurtful at one hand and we women could preserve, upkeep and upheld our modesty and purity at the other hand then we also can be loved and revered in almost every nook and corner across the world. For this we must restrain ourselves from exercising evil deeds.

So as to hammer all the evils and/or ills out of our homes and societies, we must not be an aberrant people. To be not termed as an aberrant people we must not violate or ignore the principles of the holy institution of marriage to have our homes cleared off the serious evils and/or ills.

Now we shall elucidate upon the factors as to how our character is assassinated and our modesty and purity are excruciated. When we, whether men or women, are purposelessly frequent with members of our opposite sex, the thing that is most affected is our sense of

perception. We start to faulter in our relationship with them and give birth to a word called
"Exploitation". These kinds of words are placed
in dictionary to be used at such junctures as
are being discussed here. But before that we
are enraged by our minds and our uprightness
and thoughtfulness are extenuated.

Enragement enlarges or sets free our sense
of perception, which thereafter edges our
sense of goodness out. We, then, encroach
upon all the human, familial, social and moral
barriers to be doing something wrong such as
to be expelled and lost in the oblivious jungle
of exhalement with our precious character to
be obscured and obliterated in our modesty
and purity respectively. The feedback, which
we get in return, is now, as methinks, perhaps
known to all of us.

Nothing but only that in exploiting the
members of the opposite sex we ourselves
loose or assassinate our own sound innate
character at one hand and at the other hand
we are deprived of our endowed modesty
and purity. Owing to this very reason, our well-
understood and stabilized homes reduce to
nothingness and hence severe effects on our

society with the inhabitants of all ages. That is why we have been having several open problems to which we have not been able to find any concrete solution.

Only to add some spice and surprise, some people argue that frequentation is needed and helps a lot in getting acquainted with the nature, thoughts and attitudes of the members of the opposite sex. But why do they forget the very fact that every person, whether man or woman, is a unique human being in himself/herself and thus none can match the other. Attitudes or activities, above all nature, of any two persons can never be alike or identical in any way.

Thus, everything opprobrious starts with the purposeless and meaningless frequentation with the members of the opposite sex. It is only then we start pondering over our deeds and find ourselves in a mazy situation wherein we find no one listening to or even earing for us. This is because our worthiness as a man or woman is no more. We only observe our mind desanctified, our body defiled and our soul debased. After this desanctification, defilement and debasement we are reduced to no good position and then our family, home and society at large jeer at and term us as worth a trifle.

Thereafter we live jointly and wait only to be frozen out. This is what none of us should indeed want to be. Hence we must not indulge in such miserable activities and must right now swear in so as to be invincible and inaccessible by the desanctifying, defiling and debasing gestures and promptitudes. Drug Abuse and the deadly AIDS are all the ultimate guests to these three d's i.e. desanctification, defilement and debasement. These all evils and/or ills cumulatively act behindhand and destroy our homes and society after quakingly playing havoc with them. These evils and/or ills have been having venomous effects on our children, teenagers, youths and we elders to be pushed mercilessly to a merciful situation.

Thus, for God's sake and for humanity's sake, too, we must do our best possible to hammer all these evils and/or ills out of our homes so as to be completely unaffected to be happy therein with our respective families. After peeping through the above lines the importance of the following saying increases a lot.

नगरी नगरस्येव रथस्येव रथी सदा ।
स्वशरीरस्य मेधावी कृत्येष्ववहितो भवेत ।।

i.e. "Just as a civilian or a cityman or a mu-
nicipal-man is always careful and attentive to
his duties to maintain and upkeep the city or
town and a chariot-owner or a chariot-driver
maintains and upkeeps his chariot carefully,
attentively and reasonably; similarly a witty
man or a prudent man or a judicious man or
simply a man ought to maintain and upkeep
his body judiciously and thoughtfully and
ought always to be careful and cautious in
his deeds and character."

More important and sagacious is the on-
coming saying, at the cost of repetition;

चारित्र्यं नरवृक्षस्य सुगंधि कुसुमं शुभम ।
आकर्षणं तथैवात्र लोकानां रञ्जनं महत ।।

i.e. "Character is the most beautiful, extra
ordinarily festive and fully blossomed flower
of ours being humans. Like a full blossomed
overwhelming and beautiful flower the good

**and impressive character attracts everybody toward one and pleases and impresses everyone who comes in contact."**

For, the call of the hour is that we must lead a pleasant and agreeable life with our respective life-partners and must avoid divorce so far as possible if we indeed care for ourselves, our children, the next generation, our homes and our society and the surroundings around us because only then we can expect of our children to be prospering and prosperous in the future. To keep up well with one's own life-partners, one is always advised to be patient and understanding as these outstandingly work to having good acquaintance with each other and help ease the bitter and nuisance atmosphere and the relationship.

To support this claim comes the quotation picked and chosen, "To become witty and worthy one must face one's antagonists, perfect, bold and above all make one learn how to live and cope-up well with one's opposition as they, i.e. the opposition or the antagonists, make one the hostile factors. One's wrestler strengthens one's nerves and sharpens one's skill". More or less the same kind of wrestling atmosphere has been prevailing now as, at one hand, social ills like Drug abusing and the lethal AIDS are over loading us whereas, at the other hand, only to add fuel to the fire is the increasing number of divorces and their ill-effects.

So, the present hour calls at our own respective doors to come out, join the hands up with sheer determination and co-operation and be ready to root out all these evils and/or ills completely so that they never enroot our minds, our bodies and our souls and our homes and societies again. We are accustomed to such boisterous and vociferous wrestling and at every testing moment, we have proved successful and victorious. Then why not this time? Indeed such would be the outcome this time, too.

Government of any country in any corner of the world tries its best so as to be capable of tactfully, quantitatively and qualitatively, handling the hellish and venomous atmosphere and the surroundings arising out of all these discussed evils and/or ills. Governments, all over the world, are engaged in evolving the effective and good result-oriented strategies and programmes such as to disgrace them nobly. Our scientists, sociologists, psychologists, doctors, psychiatrists, philosophers, physiologists, anthropologists and leaders are also delegated to considerately and lovingly look into the problems and reasons and then subsequently spy out the answers and measures to do away with these evils and/or ills.

They are all hopefully progressing in their respective departments and exercises. But, they will have any or complete success only if they receive our wholehearted support and succour and if not, their efforts to dismantle or comb them out will come a cropper or good-for-nothing or at least prove to be of no purpose and futile. So much so, what we are for then if everything and that too, for our good and wholly benignant to us is to be looked after by our respective Governments alone? Whereas, our own Governments have several other things and programmes in their hands to be looked into.

And hence the burden of uprooting all these evils and/or ills automatically falls upon our respective shoulders being the creator, dweller and upkeeper of the homes and so-cieties. It is our duty and an obligation, too, for we must not let their efforts go futile and prove good-for-nothing. For this, we shall have to wake others, along with ourselves, up and set about doing our best possible to bear down completely upon these evils and/or ills. This needs to be begun right now and from within our respective four walls.

For this we must correct and make ourselves upright with the help of the idea of self-restraint and then advise others to do so instead of get-ting busy in blaming–each-other and pooh-poohing-each-other syndrome and only then our governments with their delegates and authorities will have successco[14], any or complete success, in the exertions or efforts to wipe all these evils and/or ills out. Above all and over all, our character and modesty and purity are what we love and revere most and hence must anyhow be corrected, preserved and made upright.

Thus, to conclude, the pith of this book is that we are made to marry and live conviv-ially and concordantly and not that we are

---

14  The Complete Success, opposite of Fiasco.

made to follow the beaten track of divorce, i.e. marry-go-tarry-go-empty or even violate or neglect the just and pure principles of the holy institution of marriage and only then we can hope of keeping an erudite eye over ourselves, our offspring, our homes, our society and the surroundings around us at large thereby keeping all these ills i.e. Drug Abusing and the internecine AIDS (Acquired Immune Deficiency Syndrome), besides several others, almost innumerable, out of our respective doorways so far as possible to be HAPPY ADVIVUM.

# Afterword

Home is where the Heart is!

From the cradle to the grave, the importance of the Home is always there. It is here that we try to learn and unfold every bit of our life. It gives us everything that we require or desire to have to lead a life full of quantity and quality. From our grandparents to grandchildren, we try to re-live our lives seeking our pleasures and sharing our sorrows through the times. Even in the midst of the most extreme moments, favourable or unfavourable, we do not wish to be dead and rather want to live ever and ever, forever.

The Almighty has provided us with 2 ears and 1 mouth. It means we should Think twice before we Speak, or Speak less and Listen more. Less said is always better than saying too much. That leaves the audience with unsaturated hunger and too many options to ponder over. This will inculcate in us a sense of Accountability that will not only allow us to perform our duties judiciously but also vests in us the much needed right to ask for a more purposeful well-being. I leave it to the wisdom of the readers of my book to evaluate, judge and then do the needful.

The theory of Supply and Demand works everywhere, not only in Economics. Like it is said that for a market to sustain healthy and durable, there has to be a Seller and a Buyer. And both must take care of each other for the market to sustain forever. Similarly, if we know the mechanism of matching expectations, then we shall be the extremely successful people. How much should we expect from others and how much should we encourage others to expect from us? I think our common sense and prudence coupled with our education will play an important role here.

When we are born on this magnificent Earth, we seldom know or try to know the purpose of it. Why do we want to study or get educated, why do we grow up, why do we play, why do we earn, why do we marry or not marry and produce children, why do we invent so many things? Why? Ultimately each one of us has to disappear one day.

When? Why do we enjoy being here? Even in the midst of testifying circumstances; physical, monetary or otherwise.

This is an ongoing tradition for countless centuries. The Almighty too is interested in this tradition to go on and on, forever. That's why, even when some calamity strikes us, He leaves some life behind, and hope, to carry on the torch. Then why not we try to add some value and quality into whatever we do, right from our first to our last breath.

Love, and to be loved, is what we die for. We grow up for the same. To be living with love is another great achievement in our life. In love alone, we do not come across any boundary. It enables us to live a complete and fruitful life. It teaches us great lessons of life that we, otherwise, may not be able to learn at all. It gives you shocks and after-shocks as well. It gives you earthquakes, tsunamis and what not. But they are all full of lively juices and pleasures.

Marriage is what we all have to go through. Rather we wait, patiently or impatiently, for it to happen in our respective lives. It gives us license to love and be loved. It gives us license to do whatever we want to, in the name of love. It has immense capacity and potential to change the trajectory of our respective lives. It gives a new look and purpose to our lives. It can turn us into everything from nothing, depending upon how we look at it. Marriage is what makes a man a man and a woman a woman!

Marriage is the best of all lessons and consists of all proven theories (Management, Economic, Political, Social, Administrative, Educational etc.). All management jargons and lessons you can learn from it. It teaches us how to live and work as a cohesive unit. It teaches us how to surrender and sacrifice for each other and be winning always. It teaches us how much and what to expect and allow our respective life partner to expect from us. It teaches us how well to share our belongings, plenty or inadequate. It helps us to create a world of our own. So please BE Self, BE Married. This solves many of our problems. BE means Basics and Ethics.

Whatever we do, we must bear in mind the basics and ethics of it. In the current times of unpredictable moments, these two words will help us guide out of all our hardships. Basics will enable us to have our roots firmly grounded and Ethics will enable us to have good growth. BE is the best winning combination for anything and everything.

# About the Author

Being the World's original thinker-cum-writer and experiencing the kind of lives led by people around, he has felt continuously motivated to share his own tale of tells with everyone across the globe. Coming from a complex socio-cultural background, what India is all about, and besides being a voracious digester of cross sections of books and happenings around, the author is penning 3 books one after another; **Divorce 2 Divorce**, **Freedom Unfinished** and **Zero Hour**. First of his 3 books i.e. Divorce 2 Divorce is being published. Other 2 books are expected to come out in the near future, one after another.

Being first of the 3 book series, Divorce 2 Divorce, the author tries to lend to everyone an authority to lead a purposeful life of mutual happiness and achievement. Having gained first hand experiences of a life replete with multi-coloured and multi-cultured socio-economic factors, it has acted as a catalyst and given him the impetus to pen down the current book. He thinks that "Life with quality and quantity" is the most enjoyable thing to happen to everyone on the Mother Earth.

He currently lives in Dubai, UAE with his family. Dubai in UAE is another unique place of growth and interest where different races and nationalities mix and mingle, shoulder to shoulder, harmoniously giving its lifestyle a true cosmopolitan, rather Globo-politan, nature. Dubai helps you learn to lead a modern yet cultural life of discipline, happiness and achievement.

# Resources to D2D People

- www.alokkr.com

- www.divorce2divorce.info

- www.freedom2all.co.in

- Follow Alok Kr on Facebook (http://facebook.com/AlokKrIndia)

- Follow Alok Kr on twitter (http://twitter.com/AlokKrIndia)

- Always remember the most beautiful and purposeful word in the English language that is **"BE". BE means Basics and Ethics.** Whatever we do in our respective lives, we should try to always do that with this word in mind. This word can not be described in brief, rather go deep and we understand its meaning and usefulness in our day-to-day life.

www.ingramcontent.com/pod-product-compliance
Lightning Source LLC
Chambersburg PA
CBHW022252290526
45785CB00015B/718